CASH YOUR INVESTMENT

CASH YOUR INVESTMENT

How to Leverage Your College Degree into a Great First Job

S. A. EBERWEIN

BROWN BOOKS
PUBLISHING GROUP

Cash Your Investment
How to Leverage Your College Degree into a Great First Job

Brown Books Publishing Group
16250 Knoll Trail Drive, Suite 205
Dallas, Texas 75248
www.BrownBooks.com
(972) 381-0009

A New Era in Publishing®

ISBN 978-1-61254-232-4
LCCN 2015955305

Printed in the United States
10 9 8 7 6 5 4 3 2 1

For more information or to contact the author, please go to www.CashYourInvestment.com

To my wife for her patience, to my parents for their continued support, to my children, to my friends (yes, including you, R. S. K.), and, of course, to my brother, without whom this book would not be possible.

Contents

Acknowledgments

A huge thanks to Milli Brown, Kathy Penny, Derek Royal, Amanda Siegfried, Rebecka Scott, Judy Hebb, Mike Towle, Danny Whitworth, Josie Gerlach, and everyone else at Brown Books who helped make this project a reality.

Special thanks also goes to Patrick Hoffman, Jeannie Cunnion, Jamey Newberg, Michael Holmes, and Eve Mayer for their contributions, inspiration, and advice.

Introduction

During the early stages of my job search as a college senior, I had an informational interview with a friendly junior employee from a commendable firm in my targeted corporate sector. When I arrived at his office to learn the ins and outs of his business, my chaperone described his daily duties and led me on an enlightening tour of his cubicle-packed corporate domain, affectionately referred to as "the bullpen" by him and his fellow junior-level troops. Escorting me around the inner workings of the company, he introduced me to co-workers and led me through other key departments, such as the company's massive sales and trading operation, which encompassed multiple floors of the building. I made mental notes of everything along the way, which helped me later at a formal interview. Although I benefited immensely from the walk-through and picked up a barrelful of insight, smack in the middle of the experience, I distinctly remember thinking, *This is great and all, but what do I need to do to get a job here? What exactly do I need to do to get my foot in the door with a high-caliber firm like this?* Suddenly stuck on the basic problem of catching on with a superlative employer in the first place, I quickly lost interest in seeking any further details from my gracious host on his small corner of the business.

Although I greatly appreciated the exposure, I realized straightaway that I held only a faint grasp of my forthcoming senior-year job search. I had managed a commendable grade point average. I had recently wrapped up a fruitful internship with a top-drawer business. But I remained in the dark on the steps necessary for landing top-level, post-diploma employment. I knew to make use of my campus career services center to the fullest and to check in with my personal connections, but I had no definitive blueprint for securing passage into the premium end of the professional domain. Despite four years of time, effort, and money invested in higher education, and despite my lofty aims for a post-college profession, I still faced a pronounced learning curve in landing with a blue-ribbon employer.

College can educate you on economics, mathematics, English composition, science, history, humanities, and the like, plus a kaleidoscope of advanced subjects pertinent to your major, but the experience sheds only marginal light on the subject of your senior-year job search. Despite the depth of your college grounding, your tuition nets you no definitive guidebook or concrete instruction on the subject of translating your blood, sweat, and tears from the prior four years into a gainful, career-inaugurating post within the corporate arena. College comes up short in the area of properly drilling you on the nuances of getting the most out of your hard-earned degree and steering you into a rewarding full-time career.

That is not to disparage education or diminish the value of earning a college degree in any way. The university experience obviously offers a trove of benefits. College remains a prime destination for learning and personal growth—even the majority of Ivy League institutions, which maintain a staunch emphasis on education, don't offer business degrees, as might be expected. Moreover, and most importantly, although not necessarily designed to place you on a straight-line path to a premium-wage post in the professional arena, of course, school provides you with the necessary credentials to compete for a top-end job; investing in a university pedigree obviously remains a necessity if you are to access the upper end of the white-collar domain. Clearly, individuals pulling down college diplomas have the upper hand over their unschooled counterparts when it comes to getting a topflight job.

At some point, your schooling leaves off and your professional career begins. At a certain juncture, you bear the burden of taking over the reins of your future. A bachelor's degree by itself guarantees you nothing.

Of course, your undergraduate enrollment affords you access to a prime and potentially indispensable job-search resource in the form of your campus career services center, perhaps the only resource you need to link up with top employers. However, this first stop along your path to the professional sphere is not without limitation. Despite its primacy in your job-search efforts and its value to your campaign, your school job placement office remains only one field of many to mine for post-graduation opportunities.

What if your personal ambitions exceed the caliber of the offerings within your campus career services center? What if only a sparse quantity of upper-ranking firms recruit at your university during your senior year? What if your campus career services center offers none of the first-rate, entry-level positions you most covet? What if, for example, you wish to work for an established technology outfit in Silicon Valley, but no such entities recruit at your school? Topflight firms cannot realistically conduct interviews at every college campus.

Furthermore, your campus career services center remains embedded in an academic setting. Any firsthand counsel you receive regarding your future career springs from academic-ingrained voices that might be removed from the "real world" professional grid. Your school might not employ ex-corporate professionals capable of imparting primo instruction on the subject of how to conduct a successful, high-level employment search. If your campus career services center offers a mentor-type program that pairs you up with professionally established alumni and others from the white-collar workforce, take advantage of any such services. But you will likely need to take the initiative in seeking out firsthand guidance from productive professionals already in the workplace.

Investigate the full breadth of the offerings within your campus career services center. Even if you graduate from a commendable undergraduate program and enjoy access to a number of quality hiring firms, in the interest of maximizing your prospects to link up with premium employers, hunt for grade-A employment possibilities and guidance beyond the confines of your university.

With respect to my own situation, I craved first-order employment on or as close to Wall Street as possible. Endowed with a stout resume and eager to take on the rapid-fire pace of the epicenter of the financial world in Manhattan, I focused on the apex of the employment totem. Unfortunately, no upmarket employers from that sphere registered any employment opportunities at my university, nor did they recruit on my campus at all. I explored the sparse range of respectable jobs within my campus career services center and went on a smattering of safety-valve interviews close to home but remained on my own in my bid to land at a world-class firm in the City that Never Sleeps. Although I attended a sound academic institution, my university job placement office paired me up with none of the sought-after, career-inaugurating opportunities atop my wish list. Not to degrade my school or the caliber of the education I received, but my university offered little help in connecting me to my vision of the employment promised land. I had to travel off campus to chase down the preferred Wall Street employers on my radar. How did my story play out? After learning the ropes and employing the very tools I lay out in this book, with a major assist from my mentor, I found my way into an investment banking position with a world-class firm in New York City.

• • •

In the pages that follow, I break down everything you need to know to execute a bounteous quest for gainful employment. I offer background and advice on all matters pertaining to your job search, ranging from early-stage preparation to core execution strategies, to your triumphant conquest in the form of a first-rate offer of full-time employment from a well-regarded enterprise. For deeper perspective, I also provide my own firsthand experiences. I equip you with the knowledge and the tools to get the most out of your campaign and leverage your university degree into a first-class, premium-wage job.

In chapter 1, I discuss frame of mind, the most important piece of the job-search puzzle. I highlight the sheer and utter necessity of embracing an optimum mindset prior to setting sail on your critical expedition. I explain how fostering any measure of a downbeat psyche works to your detriment, while staving off any self-defeating thoughts prior to their incubation and cultivating inner conviction and positivity sets the table for a fruitful job search. Furthermore, I offer tips on polishing your disposition and conquering this crucial factor of the equation.

In chapter 2, I extol the virtues of consulting with a qualified mentor throughout your campaign. I flesh out the expertise and experience he or she brings to the table and expound upon the plethora of ways a mentor can bolster your cause. I elaborate on the profound impact my coach had on my march toward the professional sphere and also share my own positive experiences in bringing in a sound mentor.

In chapter 3, I delve into the meat and potatoes portion of the book, offering enlightenment on numerous job-search plans of attack. After leading off with a nuts and bolts discussion on campus interviewing, I dissect networking and the monumental importance of leveraging your connections to drum up opportunity. I also cover a number of other, perhaps less apparent, means of connecting with first-tier employers. These include strategies such as mining within college internships (past or present), cold calling employers, utilizing recruiters, combing through employment listings, and even contracting out your labor minus a paycheck.

Lastly, in chapters 4 and 5, I focus on interviewing and the art of the resume, respectively. Although gallons of ink have already been spilled on these two essential topics, I nevertheless offer up my own perspective, particularly after learning the ropes myself and then switching over to the other side of the recruiting equation, evaluating incoming undergraduate resumes and sizing up applicants from an employer's viewpoint.

After reading these pages and heeding my advice, I am sure you will not have to rely on your lucky rabbit's foot to successfully cash your investment in your education and land a high-paying first job after college.

Chapter 1
Master Your Mind

U pon finally reaching legal age during college, a colleague of mine eagerly set out on a tour of the local bar scene around campus. Keen on the idea of raising a few with his buddies and upgrading his prospects to mingle with appealing members of the opposite sex, he generally waded into these nighttime excursions brimming with confidence and with a discernible spring in his step. Upon his arrival at a particular hotspot on any given day, he fluidly made the rounds with the usual flock of schoolmates and also chatted up the resident bartending crew and waitstaff on shift. Of course, he and his male cohorts were always aware of any attractive young women sprinkled among the barroom populace. However, in the event he zeroed in on a particularly enticing subject, my associate invariably clammed up and retreated from his social hilltop, morphing into his own worst enemy. Even after receiving ample encouragement from his supportive co-conspirators to saunter over and introduce himself to the object of his affections, he invariably dismissed any such talk and ultimately issued the following revelation: "Nah, I'm not going over there; she's out of my league." Time and time again, he flat out refused to even entertain the idea of venturing over to any of the ladies in question in order to start a casual conversation. Needless to say, he never emerged from these outings with any phone numbers, nor with any brightened possibilities for female companionship.

Despite his unobjectionable physical appearance and engaging personality, my compatriot lacked the initiative to aim high in his social pursuits. Handcuffed by his own flagging self-confidence, particularly when expelled from his comfort zone, he self-terminated his prospects for a date. Favoring the comfortable sidelines, he altogether refrained from entering the playing field, not even to swing the bat. Rather than boldly approach any of these women for friendly conversation, he effectively deemed himself unfit to realistically compete for their affections. He checked out prior to even firing a shot.

Worse, however, he remained entirely unaware that his own mental state was dragging him down. He misguidedly subscribed to the ill-conceived notion that his fortunes with members of the opposite sex lay out of his hands, so he essentially resigned himself to an unsatisfactory social life. He failed to appreciate the complete and utter death knell his corrosive frame of mind dealt his prospects for romance.

What if, on the other hand, my colleague displayed nothing but confidence? What if, rather than abandoning ship before even leaving the dock, he fully grasped the importance of harboring a confident mindset in such scenarios and simply believed wholeheartedly in his ability to connect with ladies?

Surely he would fare exponentially better. Surely he would upgrade his odds of success. Although not necessarily foolproof or entirely impervious to failure—he may ooze assurance yet still strike out in the short term—fully embracing a confident attitude unquestionably yields greater possibilities for success.

Here lies the secret to your success.

Approach your all-important, senior-year campaign for gainful employment with a positive attitude, with confidence that you will succeed. In order to successfully navigate your end-of-college crossroads and land gainful, full-time employment in your favored field, overcome any insecurities that threaten to sabotage your operation, as in the case of my cohort. Embark upon your operation with unwavering faith in your capabilities and in your capacity to realize your career objectives.

Simply put, be the master of your mental domain. Wield the scepter over your inner kingdom, and cultivate a constitution of belief and self-assuredness.

Moreover, rebuff negativity. Acknowledge potential unfavorable outcomes, but adopt an all-around positive frame of mind that forestalls any counterproductive thoughts from infiltrating your head and potentially derailing your efforts. Fully embrace a healthy mental makeup that prevents psychological pitfalls detrimental to your campaign. Do not fall prey to any of the following pessimistic observations that all too commonly roll off the tongues of employment-seeking, graduating college seniors, either as excuses for their uninspired efforts and/or as misguided rationales for their struggles in nailing down top-end employment:

> "The economy is weak, so there really aren't any good jobs out there right now."

> "My sector really isn't hiring anyone at the moment."

> "The top firms in my field simply aren't hiring many new undergraduates this year."

"My resume isn't good enough to compete with those at the top of our class."

"I don't really interview very well, so I'm sure I'll be hard pressed to get a great job."

"I don't have the right major to land a great job in my preferred field."

"It is going to be too difficult landing the type of job I really want."

Although such statements may bear kernels of truth in many cases (for example, the economy may remain undeniably sluggish at the time of your graduation), they nonetheless stew a decidedly negative undercurrent. Unquestionably, espousing such glass-half-empty views poses no benefit and may very well jeopardize your operation. Permitting such malignancies to take root in your brain weakens your resolve and reduces your capacity to reap a fruitful job-search harvest. If you believe that any of these roadblocks, irrespective of their validity, represent insurmountable hurdles, you surely will compromise your potential and ultimately reduce your odds to secure coveted employment.

On the flip side, embracing a confident, buoyant inner disposition forecasts optimal prospects for success. Preventing self-doubt and other mental fault lines from proliferating within your cortex and embracing a more conducive view optimize your potential. Maintain the perspective that any deficiencies within your approach or outside of your control, such as any of those framed above, simply represent mere bumps in the road that you have the power to overcome. Avoid any inner impulse to assign a great deal of credence to such perceived threats to your livelihood, even if they reflect reality to a degree. At the end of the day, trust in your candidacy, in your skills, and in your ability to land a topflight position.

Unfortunately, a sizeable number of undergraduates remain in the dark on this fundamental concept. Much like my colleague at the start of the chapter, too many students sail through their college careers more or less unaware of—or simply remain uneducated on—the utmost necessity of forging a tiptop mental approach prior to embarking upon their job search. They perform in the classroom, construct decent resumes, and hone their interviewing skills but ultimately fail to develop a winning mindset to go along with their collegiate accomplishments. Lacking A-1 inner circuitry, they miscarry in locking up any measure of top-end employment, ultimately exiting from their final year of college with job-search outcomes well short of their original ambitions.

I recall a bright university classmate who typified such asymmetry. Endowed with above-average book smarts and a respectable resume, he commenced his all-important bid for full-time employment with gusto, fervently firing off his resume in numerous directions. Despite his initial thrust (and broader designs of landing a first-rate post with a distinguished firm), he flattened out shortly after takeoff. Ill-prepared for the blast of early headwinds he encountered, and also failing to reap any measure of immediate success, he abruptly sputtered, neglecting to follow up with his connections, or even with company representatives and human resources personnel from the very firms he aspired to join. Eventually, after struggling through the remainder of his listless campaign and allowing his best opportunities to set sail without him, he settled on a pedestrian position with a middling employer beneath his original standard.

My colleague possessed a commendable work ethic and laudable resume, so what went wrong? Why did he flounder so profoundly in chasing down his desired employment after achieving his goals in college? Why did he struggle to grab the bull by the horns and take full advantage of his opportunities?

When pressed on why he misstepped in communicating more reliably with his connections and the employees from the primary corporate targets on his wish list, he responded with comebacks eerily similar to the downbeat remarks I underscored previously: "Oh, I really didn't want to bother those people" and "I don't know if I would have gotten a job with those companies anyway."

My peer's eyebrow-raising remarks certainly revealed a glaring deficiency in his repertoire. Although he bore ample brainpower and demonstrated sufficient academic dexterity, at the end of the day, he simply lacked the juice to attack his post-graduation goals with any measure of sustained conviction. Like my embattled cohort at the opening of the chapter, he came up short in terms of harboring the inner certainty required to comfortably engage individuals from his favored grade of employers and even his own personal contacts. Flustered by the icy corporate shoulder, he lost his nerve and ultimately could not fully envision himself functioning within a top-end business environment, despite his inspiring start. Even after storming out of the gate, he all but dissuaded himself from further engaging any of the parties pivotal to his campaign, ultimately accepting a lesser position more reflective of his true comfort level.

In order to gain dominion over your psyche and cultivate an optimal mental approach, execute any number of utilitarian strategies. Just as you fine-tune your resume and interviewing aptitude, delve into a range of worthwhile plans of attack that bolster your disposition, challenge you, and ultimately foster inner faith in your capabilities and in your capacity to secure gainful employment.

First and foremost, maintain your awareness of the need to fully wrap your arms around an A-1 mindset. Win half the battle at the outset by simply reminding yourself on a regular basis of the need to breed and ultimately sustain an all-around positive frame of mind. Specifically, maintain unfailing inner conviction in your capabilities and in your ultimate capacity to achieve your objectives. Depending upon your level of receptiveness to such practice, engage in a handful of psyche-building exercises throughout your job search. Articulate your strong suits ("I possess a great candidacy"), your commitment to attaining your objectives ("I *will* land a great first job after graduation"), plus any other constructive comments to a mirror regularly. Alternatively, jot down these reinforcements and personal affirmations on a sheet of paper, and revisit them on occasion. At the end of the day, make a conscious decision to maintain a favorable outlook and engage in any activity that fosters an optimal mindset that hammers home the merits of your candidacy and your power to realize your ultimate employment goals.

Second, consult your mentor (see chapter 2). Call on your coach to bolster the gray matter between your ears. Enlist his or her services to not only render sage insight and guidance relevant to your plight but also to provide encouragement, instill confidence, and serve as a stabilizing force to shepherd you through the inevitable peaks and valleys that come with the territory. For example, in the event you face a generous helping of rejection at the hands of several of the firms on your radar and your spirit wanes as a result, lean on your mentor to rejuvenate your mood with a verbal elixir of revitalizing words of wisdom and encouraging counsel that steadies your mental ship.

Third, fully sharpen the two key visible aspects of your candidacy: create a dazzling resume that optimally encapsulates your undergraduate body of work, and prime your interviewing craft to the best of your ability. Unquestionably, setting sail on your expedition with these two critical pieces of the puzzle firmly in place will bolster your conviction and pump fresh air into your voyage. Employers respond favorably to candidates with well-crafted resumes who also exhibit confidence.

Fourth, ramp up your association with individuals from the professional sphere. Participate in activities that promote greater interaction with frontline professionals from the type of companies you are interested in joining. In particular, expand your level of dialogue with productive co-workers from your internship. Engage both junior and senior office personnel inside and outside your office arena, and establish a rapport with your officemates. Talk with them about topics beyond the typical office chatter and the all-business discourse that tends to dominate during normal working hours. For example, in the event an employee arranges an informal gathering outside of the workplace and cordially invites you to attend, certainly accept the invitation. Mingle with your fellow team members, and take full advantage of the opportunity to mix with the office mates in attendance, particularly within the laid-back context. Refrain from venturing into your employer's office day in, day out and performing your daily duties without exerting much effort to communicate with the seasoned professionals in your midst.

Attend company-sanctioned recruiting events on or off campus (see chapter 3). Pose pertinent questions, and actively participate in discussions fronted by the event coordinators. These events generally provide you with invaluable exposure to individuals from the professional grid.

Furthermore, participate in informational interviewing sessions, which are not formal job interviews but rather, more casual meetings with professionals (see chapter 4). In addition to gathering firsthand insight into your chosen sector, as well as individual companies, these ventures also provide opportunities to interact with your interviewing hosts on a more social level and a chance to improve your comfort level with established professionals. Above all, participate in any activity that fosters a more spirited, confident state of mind. Prior to setting out on your mission, engage in any of the above strategies or other constructive actions that eliminate self-doubt, spur confidence, improve your overall disposition, and upgrade your sense of belonging to the competitive professional ecosystem.

Conveying an A-1 mental approach simply trumps all. Despite the profound importance of spawning a standout resume and interviewing skill set, commencing your senior-year crusade with model inner architecture remains the key to attaining success on the job-search front. Fully embracing and sustaining a buoyant, self-assured, and determined frame of mind over the course of your operation represents the recipe for maximizing your possibilities to emerge from your campaign with a coveted full-time job offer with a premium employer. Candidates harboring model make-up throughout are virtually certain to fare better than their less mentally robust counterparts, including those wielding competitive resumes but lacking superior mental firepower.

If you are to take anything away from this book, realize that, above all else, your mental approach—exactly how you think—more so than any other aspect of your job search remains the critical factor in determining whether or not you ultimately succeed in obtaining a top-shelf, post-graduation job.

Action Items for Chapter 1: Master Your Mind

- Master your mental domain:
  - Rebuff negativity.
  - Embrace a confident, buoyant inner disposition.
- Maintain your awareness of the need to fully embrace an A-1 mindset:
  - Engage in mindset-bolstering exercises on a regular basis.
  - Articulate your strong suits and other constructive comments to a mirror.
  - Jot down personal reinforcements and affirmations on paper, and revisit them.
- Create a superb resume, and hone your interviewing craft to the fullest.
- Ramp up your association with individuals from the professional sphere.

Chapter 2
Utilize a Mentor

At this point, you doubtlessly embody a mixture of healthy anxiety, exhilaration, and uncertainty. You eagerly await graduation and the appealing prospect of earning your very own big-league paycheck from a top-shelf employer. However, the idea of venturing outside of your collegiate comfort zone and into the high-velocity professional working world surely chafes your nerves. Unseasoned in the white-collar arena, save for a brief cameo or two in the form of a relatively low-pressure college internship or two, you harbor no experience or wisdom to draw from to relieve your concerns. Furthermore, you have yet to take on a quest for employment of this magnitude. Consequently, you find yourself in need of direction and advisement from someone who has walked in your shoes before.

Remedy your inexperience and angst by tapping the mental stores of an individual who has subdued your plight previously. In the face of a fast-approaching graduation and the attendant wash of emotions, consult a shrewd, experienced voice from the professional arena. This could be an elder family member, colleague, or other pertinent figure who has made the transition from industrious undergraduate to gainfully employed wage earner, someone who has already endured running through the undergraduate job-search course. Recruit the services of a seasoned mentor to imbue sage insight and serve as a sounding board for your all-important campaign.

Following are numerous contributions a sound mentor brings to the table:

Frame of Mind

Above all else, your mentor firms your grip on a winning mindset. Prior to your firing off your resume or reaching out to your first prospective employer, your coach promotes your adoption of a grade-A mental approach, the primary stepping stone to your success.

Your mentor instills confidence. In order to ensure peak operating performance, he fills you with high praise, reinforcing your strong suits and praising the merits of your candidacy. Appealing to your ego, he fosters resolute inner faith in your skill set and in your ability to reel in your favored brand of post-graduation employment.

Moreover, your coach also plays the role of master motivator. As a safeguard against any letup in your fervor, he keeps you focused on the task at hand. Wary of the minefield of potential distractions you face—namely, your academics, extracurricular pursuits, and the many items bedecking your social calendar, all threats to pull you in another direction and interfere with your pursuit of the grand prize—your coach fixes your gaze on the bigger picture. For example, prior to your engaging any discerning corporate screeners, she administers an inspiring pep talk that ignites a healthy flame under your seat. Promoting sustained vigilance and metronome-like consistency on your part, he or she pushes you to keep your foot on the gas and to remain steadfast in your pursuit of your employment Holy Grail.

Lastly, your adviser serves as a stabilizing influence. When the inevitable bumps in the road crop up and threaten to subvert your spirit, your coach picks you up. In the event you face a heavy dose of rejection at the hands of one or a number of the five-star employers atop your wish list and your mental ship risks running aground as a result—certainly not an uncommon event, even for the most headstrong graduating, college-senior job seekers—your coach steps in and gives you a much-needed shot in the arm. Putting the brakes on any ruinous downshifts in your mood, your coach imparts inspiring remarks and recharges your batteries. She offers her assurances of your imminent landing with a distinguished employer, despite the setback. Keeping you on the right track, she bolsters your morale and keeps you focused on finding your next opportunity.

Interviews

Your mentor polishes your interviewing skills. Prior to releasing you into the white-collar interviewing wild to lock horns with the corporate beasts on your interviewing slate, he taps his mental reservoir of expertise and sharpens your ability to shine under the cross-examination heat lamp.

First off, your coach doles out expedient industry insight. Drawing from her own experience and understanding, she bestows sector- and company-specific intelligence above and beyond the rudimentary information found online and within other public, readily available resources. She capacitates you with the necessary command of your sector to handle exacting corporate cross-examiners and their precise lines of questioning.

Preparing me for my cardinal interviews during senior-year interviewing season, my mentor topped off my mental storage tanks with up-to-date, industry inside scoop. Versed in my targeted field after having served time there himself after college, he enlightened me on office cultures, corporate footing within the larger business picture, and specific business strategies, such as employer designs of gathering greater shares of the industry revenue pie. He gave me the lay of the land on the principal players in the space, both substantial and niche, and foreign and domestic, a number of which were on my senior-year interviewing docket. He also mixed in his own views on prevailing industry trends and other relevant tidings, which I diligently added to my company-specific notes. He shed light on employee lifestyles with respect to hours worked and the possible sacrifices I would have to make with regard to my work-life balance, given the heavy workload I faced. He also offered up his own take on employer expectations and the qualities these firms look for in fresh, incoming undergraduate recruits like me. He even educated me on my anticipated path upon my hire at one of the acclaimed firms on my radar—he spoke of my enrollment into a formal, company training program for fresh undergraduate rookies and subsequent placement into my particular area of the firm. Lastly, he offered up a handful of astute questions for me to pose to my cross-examiners.

Second, your coach metes out instruction on your in-person aptitude. Attuned to the nuances of successful interviewing, after having conquered her own brushes with unforgiving corporate screeners, she dispenses specific tips on such important matters as your face-to-face demeanor, eye contact, attire, etc. Moreover, she preps your responses to challenging interviewer fastballs. She sharpens your poise and teaches you how to tame daunting corporate interviewers. She outfits you with the necessary knowledge to effectively convey your insight and preparedness for the shark-infested corporate waters that await you and to ultimately thrive under the corporate interviewing floodlight.

Lastly, your mentor spearheads your mock interviewing effort. In order to acclimate you to the high-pressure interviewing environment, your coach recreates the challenging corporate interrogation machine and puts you to the test. Assuming the form of a hardened, real-life cross-examiner from one of the companies on your radar, he takes you to task on everything from the contents of your resume to your understanding of the industry. Subsequently, he enlists the services of competent third parties from the professional sphere to get in on the action and run you through additional mock interviews. Given his experience and extensive contact list, your mentor may be your best resource when it comes to bringing in additional, qualified outside help.

Resume

Your mentor plays a vital role in the crafting of your resume. Versed in the subject after having already navigated the choppy interviewing job-search seas herself, she augments your resume-drafting process in numerous ways.

First and foremost, your guide imparts precise direction on all facets of the resume-crafting game. Drawing from his own mastery, he draws up a cohesive skeleton for you to work from. He also lays out clear-cut guidelines with respect to your content, cosmetics, and general flow. Moreover, he tailors his instruction to your targeted strain of employer, particularly advantageous in the event you aim for a gainful future with a select group of companies or within a particular sector.

Second, your mentor rounds up model resumes for you to pattern your work after. After laying down fundamental guardrails, she volunteers a copy of her own presentation and, capitalizing on her wealth of contacts, connects you with a batch of real-life, gold-standard resumes from successful graduating college seniors of years past, namely those professionals who successfully translated their undergraduate experiences into frontline full-time careers.

Third, your guide presides over your editing and revising efforts. Once you churn out a competent preliminary draft, your adviser, serving as your first line of defense, takes a step back and renders a full diagnosis of your work. After sizing up your composition and volunteering any suggestions, he consults his contact list and brings in others to further fine-tune your efforts, akin to your mock-interviewing refinement. He recruits astute third parties from the professional sphere proficient in effective resume construction to lend their expertise and offer up additional feedback, provided you adhere to my proposed script and open up your efforts to additional outside observation. He then changes gears and filters through the inbound commentary, endorsing that which merits consideration and discarding the feedback that offers only negligible or no meaningful upgrade.

During my junior year of college, I took a first crack at executing a proper resume. After cobbling together my budding portfolio of university credentials and pre-graduation work experience and then shaping these highlights of the prior academic years into what I considered a sound configuration, I handed over my handiwork to my mentor for a checkup. After taking in that raw first offering, much to my chagrin, my coach unfortunately returned to me shortly after with a "Sorry, try again," clearly underwhelmed by my venture into resume building. My document had a long way to go before reaching anywhere near blue-ribbon status.

My mentor explained that, considering my lofty post-graduation ambitions, I required an electric composition to fend off the fierce competition I faced for the in-demand type of employment I desired. Unfortunately, I had put together an arrangement that fell far short of the target. Devoid of the necessary brawn and bite, my first attempt simply failed to measure up; my one-pager lacked any measure of star quality and appeared incapable of generating any buzz in its present form. Coming up with a product that took after the paucity of Resume B more so than the exuberance of Resume A (see pages 144–147), I needed to rack my brain for additional achievements and data points to inject into my body of work. I needed to beef up my content and add another coat of polish. I boasted a commendable grade point average, a promising internship, and a burgeoning ledger of constructive extracurricular involvement, but uninitiated in the business of effective resume composition, I missed the mark in capturing my credentials in anywhere near optimal fashion. Despite my quality content, my first draft came out looking very much the part of an amateur.

However, after conferring with my mentor, I gave my resume a much-needed face-lift. Heeding his instruction and modeling my work in the vein of the sample resumes he had sent my way, including his own one-pager and the sterling resume of one of his successful colleagues, I expounded on my subject matter, plugged in additional savory filling, fine-tuned my layout, and tightened up my word choice. Outfitted with a deeper understanding of the task at hand after several tune-up sessions with my mentor, I shored up my trouble spots and reshaped my underwhelming initial effort into a top-end formulation on par with the best of my fellow graduating seniors.

Needless to say, my mentor tuned me in to the art of effective resume building in a big way. After sitting down with him on several occasions and subjecting my work to numerous revisions, I eventually sharpened my document into a competent piece. A year later, in advance of graduation and senior-year interviewing season, I had grown considerably more adept at effective resume configuration. I engineered a stout, well-executed summation of my four-year university run that differentiated me from my peers and facilitated my entry into the interviewing dens of a host of quality employers. A prime font of resume wisdom and expertise, my coach taught me much more than the textbook information I had previously dissected.

Oversight

Your coach lends an attentive, omnipresent eye to all of your efforts. Over the course of your operation, your mentor supplies sweeping oversight and direction that backstops your campaign. Riding herd on you, she maintains a firm, ever-present grip on your situation. She keeps an open line of communication with you. She insists that you stay in touch and keep her posted on your progress. Until you pin down your preferred brand of employment, your coach ensures a smooth-sailing ship, or as smooth a sailing ship as possible given the circumstances, and safeguards against any needless, avoidable deficiencies in your approach. Rather than dispensing helpful instruction at the outset and promptly decamping, leaving you to go at it alone, your coach stays involved throughout your ordeal.

Amid my own senior-year employment quest, I remained in near-constant contact with my mentor. Taking full advantage of his experience and his accessibility, I sought out his input repeatedly and bounced questions and ideas off of him aplenty. Making time for me despite his busy schedule, he checked in on me at regular intervals throughout my adventure, particularly when, in his opinion, he was not receiving enough of my regular check-in telephone calls. Staying abreast of my situation, he doled out guidance as he saw fit. Moreover, he asked a lot of questions, quizzing me on my resume disseminations, everyday employment inquiries, and follow-up correspondence with contacts and suitors. A tower of strength and positive all-around force for my campaign, my coach undergirded my efforts until I finally booked my first top-shelf offer of full-time employment.

Candid Perspective

In taking a front-row seat on your express train to the front lines of the professional arena, your guide picks up a vested interest in your success. Your biggest fan and most ardent supporter, she shares in your disappointment when the inevitable snags derail your progress and, on the flip side, revels in your zeal and feeling of accomplishment when the ball finally rolls in your favor and you pull off your tour de force.

His skin in the game no doubt serves you well. Intent on getting the most out of you, he doles out pure, unadulterated advisement and analysis that keeps you pointed in the right direction. Sugarcoating nothing, he dispenses only candid, pointblank criticism that cuts to the heart of the matter and elevates your game. Your best and perhaps only legitimate source of objective, thought-out observation, he tells you exactly what you need to do and which moves you need to make to put your best foot forward as you scale the job-search summit.

My own coach dished out nothing but frank judgment from the get-go. Sparing no contents of my bag of tricks from his scrutiny, he laid on raw, unabashed feedback that encompassed every aspect of my campaign. Although he piled on the praise and harped on my many positives when warranted, he also shed the kid gloves and challenged me when necessary. He chopped up my first go at a resume. He picked apart my in-person presentation after witnessing my initial interviewing skills for the first time. He threw down the gauntlet and pushed me to go all out at all times. If, in his judgment, I failed to put forth my best effort or if I dropped the ball in any way—for example, not following up with contacts or company point persons in a timely enough fashion according to his standard—he did not hesitate to call me out and get in my ear. Holding nothing back, my coach cut to the chase and got right to the point when it came to highlighting my areas in need of improvement. Although I did not always appreciate his blunt brand of criticism, particularly during my dry patches, he tightened up my candidacy and my methods. No question his forthright style proved to be the best formula for success.

No one else weighs in in such upfront fashion. No one else cuts to the heart of the matter and lays on such explicit, shoot-from-the-hip coaching that brings out your best. Wishing to chip in but not necessarily risk ruffling any feathers, other less-invested individuals may not be as forthcoming with their opinions. For instance, secondary contacts and less-familiar acquaintances not as close to your situation will be less inclined to dispense pointed feedback. Not fully comfortable with the idea of telling you what to do or shining a torch on your weak spots, they may tread too lightly and refrain from doling out the bare-bones, undiluted opinion you need to rectify any holes in your swing and reap a fruitful job search. Your mentor, on the other hand, given her equity in your undertaking, dives in and squeezes every last drop out of you.

So, what makes for a great mentor? What kind of coach should you look for? Settle on a familiar face from the front lines of the professional arena, preferably in your targeted sector, not far removed from his or her own ambitious trekking through the corporate interviewing safari. Target someone with a year or more of service time under his or her belt and who is keen on the idea of mentoring your approach. Focused on your plight and familiar with your situation after having dealt with your predicament before, this person stands ready to furnish apt direction and serve as your coordinator until you find your way into a quality employer.

In the event you struggle to unearth anyone in particular who fits all of these criteria, settle on your best option. In light of the fact that you remain at the mercy of the realistic possibilities at your disposal, select an individual that, although not necessarily ideal in every respect, may nonetheless contribute quality fosterage and advice. Look for an individual who brings balance to your situation and ultimately bolsters your employment prospects.

For example, if your number-one choice checks out in all areas with the lone, glaring exception that he or she draws paychecks from a sector outside of your targeted field, bring him or her into the fold anyway. Although not exactly a prime wellspring of industry-specific intelligence, this person may nonetheless bring a lot to the table. He may still firm up your mental approach. She may still fine-tune your resume. This consultant may still upgrade your ability to curry favor with interviewers. Seek out your industry-specific education elsewhere, such as through informational interviews, and implore him or her to preside over your efforts and show you the way. Despite not being the be-all and end-all educator on all topics, he or she may very well make for a quality mentor, supplying favorable superintendence that undergirds your enterprise and leads you through the undergraduate job-search jungle.

If still no one in particular stands out above the rest, or you have no obvious front-runner to choose from, utilize a combination of mentor types to assume the role and lend their expertise as needed. Rather than rely on a sole, less-than-ideal contributor to seize the reins, seek out guidance on multiple fronts. Consult with one individual for resume and interviewing tips. Approach another for encouragement and psychological support. Gather the inside scoop on your industry and on your compass of preferred corporate destinations from someone else. Iron out the x's and o's of your overall game plan with assistance from yet another figure. You need not field all of your coaching from only one primary resource.

In fact, solicit A-plus input wherever able. Irrespective of your success in nailing down a principal chief to take the lead, gain perspective and coaching from any relevant figures you encounter en route to the corporate frontier. For example, if a colleague introduces you to a seasoned, well-regarded associate from his professional circle, take full advantage of the opportunity to forge a connection and pick his brain. Assail him with thoughtful questions, in a respectful and courteous way, of course, and heed any profitable words to the wise he passes along. Gather insight from anyone in a position to impart wisdom along your path to the professional arena.

That being said, turn a deaf ear to any bad information that throws you off course or bends your post-college arc. Upon learning of your plight, a number of outside observers, such as elders, acquaintances, and experienced professionals, may eagerly chime in and volunteer their two cents unsolicited. Although pure in intention, they may not necessarily relay fitting counsel. Unfamiliar with your situation or ill-equipped to impart timely navigation on all topics, they may not necessarily advance anything of note or anything on point that harmonizes with your objectives. Some individuals may convey helpful direction on one subject but then veer off course and offer up something counterproductive or even injurious. When on the receiving end of any such noise, particularly if borderline or coming from an uneven source, proceed with a selective ear and filter out any racket that runs counter to sound judgment in light of your aims or that steers you down the wrong path. If in doubt, run any such suspect input by a trusted third party or other credible mentor type already in your corner.

One of my colleagues from the graduating class a year behind mine faced such a situation at the beginning of her campaign. During a career strategy session with her university guidance counselor amid her senior year, her adviser, upon picking up a hint of uncertainty regarding her pupil's preferred career path, suggested that she interview with advertising firms, an out-of-left-field notion, to say the least.

Upon hearing the haphazard recommendation, I scoffed at the idea straight away. My compatriot, a bright, self-starting business major, coveted a fast-paced opportunity in the business arena, such as consulting or banking, but she remained unsure of exactly which type of post in particular she should pursue. She never expressed an interest in the advertising sector and simply needed to pare down her options from the broader business sphere; she certainly did not need to be nudged in a different direction entirely. Aware of her preferences—much more so than the uninformed voice in her ear—I pointed out that marketing sector salaries generally come in at the lower end of the pay scale, particularly relative to the more hotly contested fields she had given prior consideration. I suggested that, given her original line of thinking, she only consider opportunities in advertising if she had come off her original leanings and now favored advertising as a legitimate possibility, something I knew not to be the case. The next time she met with her campus adviser, she brought up the subject of her post-graduation career launch and mentioned the salary discrepancy between advertising and her first-choice options. Appallingly, her counselor responded that she had not given much thought to the underlying economics of the situation.

Although in a position of influence, the university staff member doled out reckless guidance that was not appropriate for this individual. Rather than get a feel for my impressionable associate and then tailor her suggestions accordingly before reaching any conclusions and dispensing shoddy advice, she irresponsibly offered up a snap, ill-fitting recommendation that flat out pointed my colleague in the wrong direction. Needless to say, my associate was better off allowing the inexpedient counsel to enter in one ear and out the other.

Your mentor impacts your job search in a profoundly positive way. An invaluable asset to your high-stakes operation, she contributes on many levels. She facilitates your cultivation of an A-1 mindset. She buffs your resume and improves your interviewing dexterity. She lends sound judgment and expertise. She nurtures your approach and bolsters your marketability to topflight employers. She cleans up your act and upgrades your possibilities to reap a bountiful job-search harvest. Teaming up with a shrewd mentor conceivably represents the difference between landing your favored brand of post-graduation employment or struggling through an uneven job search and settling for less.

My mentor polished virtually every aspect of my campaign. A brimming fountain of knowledge and wisdom, particularly when factoring in his background in my sector and comparable voyage to the professional world, he geared me up for the all-important task at hand. He mapped out a prudent plan of attack. He fine-tuned my inner architecture, keeping my mental turbine running at a high level and cementing my conviction in my ability to compete for my brand of employment pay dirt. He clued me in on the central tenets of effective resume composition and kicked the caliber of my resume up a monumental notch. He coached up my interviewing skills, psyching me up before my auditions, fine-tuning my in-person agility, and shelling out spot-on industry perspective, a huge boon to my presentation during my face-to-face meetings with exacting interrogators. Last but certainly not least, he proved to be my most profitable liaison to the corporate world. Granting me invaluable access to his robust contact list, he opened a lot of doors. He facilitated my introduction to multiple key contributors who expedited my procurement of coveted interviews with the esteemed firms on my radar. One of these individuals, after putting in a good word and passing my resume up his company chain of command, turned out to be my golden ticket. His maneuvering vaulted me past the stream of undergraduate resumes flowing into the company and led me to prime interviewing opportunities with his employer. Although I experienced resume-referral success elsewhere, he led me to my first top-shelf offer of employment.

With a strong mentor in my corner, I made the interviewing rounds with a number of the top suitors on my wish list, something not entirely possible otherwise. Augmenting my efforts and letting me in on his trade secrets, my mentor made a successful job search possible. He showed me the ropes. Although I did my part and put in the time necessary to harvest a fruit-bearing job search, he took me under his wing and flattened my learning curve considerably. Given his deep-seated impact on my operation, my mentor obviously played a vital role in my success (he used to joke that he remained entitled to a cut of my future earnings).

Had I not sought out my mentor's advice, I surely would have faced a considerably steeper hill to climb. Had I not sought out this indispensable voice in my ear to lead the way, I surely would have traversed a very different, and potentially lesser, path to my chosen profession. Teaching me everything he knew, my mentor remains a prime reason for my writing this book.

Action Items for Chapter 2:
Utilize a Mentor

- Identify a familiar, frontline professional from your targeted sector keen on the idea of mentoring your approach.
- Settle on your best option.
- Utilize a combination of mentor types, if necessary.
- Turn a deaf ear to bad advice.

Chapter 3
Conduct an Exhaustive Job Search

After studying diligently for four years, successfully completing a dynamic, resume-buttressing internship, and deftly crafting the relevant highlights of your experiences into a polished final resume, you nonetheless remain at a critical juncture. Despite the seemingly endless undergraduate grind you have already endured, paramount heavy lifting remains. With your future on the line, the time has finally arrived for you to fully immerse yourself into your all-important task at hand, the critical outcome of which determines your immediate occupational destiny. In the face of your impending graduation and imminent venture into the professional working world, the time has come at last for you to scour the landscape for a dynamic employment opportunity that lays the groundwork for a robust, career-flowering future after college.

In order to fully realize your objectives and emerge from your senior-year operation with a choice offer of full-time employment in hand, adhere to an ambitious, multifaceted formula for success. Execute an enterprising, leave-no-stone-unturned master plan of attack in which you drop multiple lines in the water at once and thoroughly explore the full range of job-search channels, including atypical avenues in certain instances. At the end of the day, hitting it from all angles and aggressively investigating the full corporate expanse for full-time employment enables you to dictate the terms of your post-diploma fate and avert any possibility of settling for subpar employment after graduation.

Prior to wading into your grand operation, however, first restructure and rebalance your everyday routine. Throughout the first several semesters of college, your career concerns largely remained on the back burner while your academics, internship commitments, and extracurricular activities monopolized the lion's share of your time. With your university swan song now in full swing, however, your hierarchy of priorities has undoubtedly shifted away from coursework and extramural endeavors and toward all elements relevant to your job search. Accordingly, you can no longer confine your daily routine solely to your academic responsibilities (including major classroom assignments and preparation for critical examinations) and your nonacademic involvements that, up until now, rounded out your agenda each day. Now that the procurement of a full-time job has clearly become your chief concern, the time has come at last for you to dial back your scholastic focus and bump each of these elements one rung down your priority ladder.

Of course, that is not to say you should entirely neglect the non-job-search obligations on your plate at present; you certainly need not obsessively devote yourself to a maniacal, around-the-clock job hunt. Forge ahead with your coursework, and sustain your social calendar and your involvement in extracurricular activities, time permitting. However, avoid the natural tendency to continue along the same academic-centric path of the prior four years, and do not allow your regular undergraduate schedule to distract you from the pursuit of your post-graduation objectives. For example, in the event you procure a coveted interview with an esteemed employer that unfortunately falls on the same day as a critical classroom examination, rather than procrastinate preparing for your interview in favor of the test, prepare for the interview prior to fully immersing yourself into your textbooks.

After you have already more or less nailed down your final grade point average, fulfilled your internship obligations, and participated in a host of other constructive, resume-building activities, elevate any and all things job search-related to priority status.

Simply put, see the forest for the trees. You did not enroll in college solely to score dazzling marks in the classroom. You also did not enlist strictly to enrich the gray matter within your cranium. Nor did you matriculate in order to gain access to raucous campus parties or to maintain fraternization continuity with your age demographic beyond high school. You did not grind through four intensive years of academic exertion because you lacked viable career options after high school, nor because you aspired to simply kill time until your lucky lottery numbers provided a fantastic financial windfall (at least I hope not). Make no mistake: you signed up for four years of the scholastic meat grinder in order to garner access to the premium end of the professional employment spectrum. You signed up to maximize your future earning power. You signed up because, with rare exception, candidates boasting only a high school diploma simply cannot realistically pull down the same caliber of employment as their college-degree-wielding counterparts.

The collegiate odyssey generally bestows a dynamic and rewarding experience, and you should certainly enrich and enjoy the adventure as much as possible. However, considering its immense costs in terms of both financial resources and time, why even earn a bachelor's degree in the first place if you ultimately flounder in sufficiently exploiting the ripe opportunities it affords? Why invest appreciable sums of money, time, and personal exertion into the higher educational experience only to fumble in translating your investment into a rewarding post-college career?

Of course, no one wishes to graduate only to queue up at the local unemployment office. Nevertheless, scores of students fail to sufficiently map out an operative blueprint, navigating the collegiate waters without the necessary preparation. Despite the clear motivation behind the push to obtain a university-refined skill set, remarkable quantities of undergraduates coast through their university tenures without grasping the profound importance of contriving an effective game plan for their post-commencement futures. Fully caught up in their academics and other day-to-day affairs, or simply unfazed by their own lack of preparation for the professional world, they leave little time for contemplating their post-diploma fates in advance. They may, then, arrive at graduation painfully destitute of any legitimate employment prospects and without any meaningful post-graduation direction at all. Amazingly, they ostensibly maintain that fortune will simply cross their paths eventually and they need only remain patient until a ripe opportunity falls into their laps.

Perhaps worse, another segment of undergraduates achieves excellence within the classroom and appears destined for greatness after college yet ultimately struggles to successfully translate their academic prowess into fruit-bearing employment once the diplomas are finally in hand. Wholly unable to conceptualize the paramount bigger picture, these students study zealously, accrue productive pre-graduation work experience in many cases, and author passable final resumes, yet arrive at the university finish line in May entirely unprepared for the full order of steps necessary to connect with top-shelf jobs after graduation. Consequently, they emerge from their schooling one-dimensional and ensnared in the same precarious position as their less-gifted and less-studious university counterparts—diploma in hand but entirely devoid of any favorable employment opportunities in their immediate futures and with only meager or no post-college direction at all.

This brings to mind a bright but ultimately shortsighted colleague from my graduating class who neatly fits this mold of "intelligent" student. Exceedingly persistent with respect to his academics, he strove for and ultimately achieved unsurpassed marks within the classroom. Furthermore, in a bit of a departure from the prototypical "intelligent" pupil hung up on simply making the grade, he gained entry into a couple of modest honors clubs on campus (even attaining the presidency in one in particular) and also landed a respectable internship with a local financial services firm prior to graduation, all seemingly secured with the intention of bolstering his final undergraduate resume.

Although academically proficient and seemingly bound for success after college, my classmate struggled to convert his five-star university achievement into prosperity at the next level. Naively relying on only his own modest knowledge of effective resume construction, he prepared a lackluster presentation of his candidacy on paper, bereft of any meaningful depth, which insufficiently highlighted his undergraduate credentials. It could not realistically compete with the resumes of the elite performers at the top of our graduating class, particularly for the prime, entry-level opportunities on virtually every ambitious student's radar. Moreover, he struggled to arrange interviews of any significance, certainly none with any of the distinguished firms on the wish lists of the stars of our graduating class, and he even stumbled through the pinch of pedestrian interviews he had managed to arrange. Ultimately, after falling behind his peers, drifting through an uneven job search, and never establishing any real momentum, he came to a sputtering halt, citing an inability to "locate any top-notch companies who are hiring." With white flag hoisted firmly and tail tucked meekly between his legs, he "did the best he could" and eventually settled on a glorified, semiclerical position in the back offices of the financial services firm he previously interned for. Perhaps most unfortunate, however, rather than gaze in the mirror and flag any deficiencies within his approach, he absurdly blamed his inability to corral any measure of first-rate employment on a stagnant employment market and a corresponding shortage of viable undergraduate employment opportunities—hardly an accurate portrayal of reality at the time.

My textbook-conquering colleague seemingly embodied a sound fusion of brainpower and work ethic. So, what went wrong? Why did he blunder so impressively in his bid to secure a laudable, post-graduation position? Why did his undergraduate achievement fail to translate into success on the job-search front?

At the end of the day, my beleaguered associate committed a fatal error. Although he hit the books with interminable fervor, mustered a banner grade point average, and even supplemented his scholastic vigor with relevant work experience and involvement in extracurricular activities, he nonetheless failed to make out the forest for the trees. Despite his laudable efforts to top off his studies with productive non-coursework-related endeavors and to put together a well-rounded undergraduate ledger, for all intents and purposes, he subscribed to the complete and total eminence of academic supremacy. He lacked the wisdom to craft a cohesive post-diploma game plan. He maintained an unremitting emphasis on his grades up until graduation and permitted his preoccupation with classroom excellence to more or less supersede all else, simply to preserve his sterling final grade point average. As a result, he lapsed in framing any measure of a firm outline for his post-academia future.

Of course, the truly brilliant pupils, those deserving of the "intelligent" label, wisely avert such ruinous errors in judgment. In full appreciation of the bigger picture, they shrewdly punctuate their scholastic credentials with foresight. With full understanding of the fact that the clearance of academic measuring sticks simply remains a means to an end, they rightly regard their classroom diligence, although vitally important, as only a singular step in the process of attaining topflight employment rather than viewing it as the be-all and end-all of college. They not only excel within the classroom but also draw up cohesive outlines for their futures that cover all of the steps necessary to successfully leverage their undergraduate elbow grease into enviable foundations within the corporate frontier.

A bounteous employment harvest hinges profoundly on your execution of an aggressive, all-encompassing strategy. Cap your four-year undergraduate track record with a driving, manifold plan of attack in which you thrust several irons in the fire at once and maximize your odds of success. Neglect to flesh out any such scheme, on the other hand, and you surely risk bridging the collegiate finish line devoid of any promising opportunities, akin to the wedge of "intelligent" undergraduates and the knot of blasé, underprepared students meandering through their college tenures that I described previously.

Of course, underpinning such counsel lay the fact that your job-search resolution remains far from etched in stone. Although you have already penned the narrative on your university tour—you have more or less nailed down your final college grade point average, fulfilled your internship obligations or some other type of relevant field experience, and applied the finishing touches to your final undergraduate resume—your post-college destiny remains a blank page, entirely in your hands. You harbor the power to attack your operation with unmatched ferocity and to outwork the majority of your fellow graduating college seniors regarding your persistence and resourcefulness.

Put another way, the caliber of employment you ultimately reel in remains independent of your level of undergraduate performance to a meaningful degree. Although graduating from a stellar academic institution with topflight grades and premium work experience undoubtedly improves your marketability to employers, differentiating yourself from your interviewing competition with respect to your vigor and tenacity on the job-search front remains the key to success. In the event you roll out an imperfect resume, or, perhaps more accurately, a resume that fails to stand out among those of the upper crust of your fellow graduating college seniors, you may yet successfully pull down a great career-inaugurating post; a less-than-perfect presentation on paper does not automatically preclude you from realizing your employment objectives. Persistence on the job-search front conceivably levels the playing field and narrows the gap between your candidacy and those of the resume-formidable all-stars at the top of your class. Ambition, initiative, and enterprise usurp university credentials any day of the week in successfully completing your favored vocational end game after commencement.

Unquestionably, the fireball undergraduates who pound the pavement and turn over every stone in their employment-hunting pursuits ultimately harbor the greatest potential to connect with the premium opportunities.

On the eve of my own christening within the professional grid after commencement, my new employer teed up a casual social mixer at company headquarters in order for my new co-workers and me to get acquainted with one another and also to interact with the human resources personnel and other staff pertinent to our recruitment into the firm. At some point over the course of the reception, I engaged a particularly impressive fellow new recruit, and I lucidly recall the crux of that first conversation between us (we subsequently worked in close proximity to one another within the firm and got to know each other quite well). After exchanging initial pleasantries and talking about our home-towns and university backgrounds, my newly acquainted peer proceeded to describe her particular path to our present destination.

Exceedingly goal oriented and supremely confident in her abilities, she explained that after earning solid grades in col-lege, rotating through not one but two top-shelf internships, and immersing herself in numerous on- and off-campus activities, she eagerly set her grand plan in motion to secure entry into a premium tier of the professional expanse. As soon as the ink had dried on her final resume, she launched a fervent campaign to blanket the landscape with copies of her presentation on paper. Moreover, in addition to taking full advantage of the range of interviewing opportunities at her university career services center and networking aggres-sively, she also canvassed virtually every upper-tier firm not already actively recruiting at her school—despite the fact that she harbored ample conviction in her campus interview-ing opportunities and networking skills. Ultimately, after machine gunning her resume off in all manner of directions and sweeping through the full corporate landscape far and wide via various plans of attack, she lined up interviews with an assortment of top-end employers and elicited multiple enticing offers before finally accepting the frontline offer from our mutual employer.

My associate achieved academically and also put together a compelling presentation of her candidacy on paper. How-ever, most importantly, she differentiated herself from her peers profoundly in her sheer and utter determination and in her ability to succeed. She did not take things slowly and embark upon her campaign at a merely moderate or leisurely pace, nor did she relax her persistence to any degree or simply pursue her goals in passive fashion. She did not limit herself to interviewing only on campus or only when evident opportunities arose, and she did not allow the outcomes of these to fully play out before looking into other avenues. Instead, she hit the ground running and stalked her career objectives with a vengeance, easing off the gas only after securing a firm invitation on par with her personal standard.

This is the type of persistence and resolve you should emulate in your own employment-hunting exertions. Unless you graduate from the top school in the country, boast a perfect resume, and are assured a primo spot within an elite employer, roll up your sleeves, and hit it from all angles in the manner of my plutonium-fueled colleague.

Furthermore, keep your foot on the gas. Like my peer, keep the pedal to the metal irrespective of the circumstances. Even if you experience a measure of early success with certain employers and appear well on your way, any immediate triumph in picking up meetings with potential employers obviously comes with no guarantees. Early successes may not necessarily translate into firm offers of employment. So, maintain a high-octane clip regardless of potential opportunities seemingly within reach until nailing down a concrete offer to your liking.

For example, if your initial employment inquiries elicit a largely favorable response, and you earn several decent first-round meetings as a result, don't rest on your laurels and slow your stride to any degree; march your operation forward full tilt, and continue to prowl for other opportunities as you wait for these early courtships to play out.

Unfortunately, a great number of undergraduates fall into bad habits and fail to exercise such practical wisdom. After lining up promising early-round interviews or, in certain instances, after merely having productive, preliminary conversations with prospective employers, some students promptly relax their exertions and temporarily halt their momentum, naively assuming that at least one of their budding courtships with employers is sure to turn out in their favor. They unwisely squander precious time by effectively placing all of their eggs in one basket. Although they may very well wind up with an offer from these initial interviewing opportunities, surely they would be best served by sustaining their drive and continuing to search out other possibilities, expanding their potential opportunities while they wait to hear back.

Map out a cohesive overall strategy ahead of time, and adhere to it without deviation. Prior to diving headfirst into the all-important task at hand, catalog the job-search avenues most relevant to your situation, rank them in more or less descending order of importance, and then canvass accordingly. For example, if you attend a modest, under-the-radar academic institution, and, as a result, the caliber of companies actively recruiting at your university comes in beneath your personal bar, look at other plans of attack first. Moreover, if you maintain a bevy of personal connections, and this invaluable edge over your employment-seeking competition represents your best bet to connect with the first-rate employers atop your wish list, lean on these resources before spinning your wheels and chasing down the marginal opportunities at your campus career services center.

That is not to say that you should approach your hierarchy of strategies in entirely mutually exclusive fashion. Instead, get the ball rolling within a particular plan of attack—for example, dispense copies of your resume and initiate correspondence with the appropriate parties. Before fully exhausting a specific channel, advance on to the next potential source of opportunity and explore other avenues. Following a strictly sequential plan has the potential to waste time while you wait for results to fully unfold from your initial efforts. The process of lining up first-round interviews and awaiting return correspondence often occurs at a molasses-slow pace, so simply keep your operation moving along, and delve into other job-searching channels in businesslike fashion. You need not entirely deplete a particular job-search approach prior to shifting gears and routing your focus elsewhere. There is always something you could be working on to upgrade your employment prospects and advance your campaign.

• • •

In the following sections, I expound upon and offer instruction on a full array of viable employment-scouting plans of attack. Presented in more or less descending order of importance—ranging from conventional to ambitious, outside-the-box, means-to-an-end strategies that you may not have considered previously—this weighted spectrum of job-search avenues, although not all of which necessarily pertain to your specific set of circumstances, more or less represents a wide-ranging field guide of options for you to pry into as you set forth on your all-important, senior-year campaign.

Action Items for Chapter 3:
Conduct an Exhaustive Job Search
Getting Started

- Rebalance your everyday routine.
- See the forest for the trees.
- Execute an ambitious, multifaceted plan of attack.
  - Hit it from all angles.
  - Keep your foot on the gas.
  - Adhere to a cohesive strategy.
  - Rank your job-search avenues, and canvass accordingly.

Interviewing on Campus

Assuming you remain on track for a conventional spring graduation, your career search should generally commence early to mid-senior year in the form of first-round interviews on your university grounds. As early as a few weeks into your final year of college, a slew of businesses from a smorgasbord of sectors, including finance, technology, health care, etc., register their entry-level employment openings at your campus. After fielding resumes from graduating seniors, these businesses arrive at your university doorstep in the weeks that ensue in order to sit down with and evaluate fresh candidates, particularly in instances in which the interviewing companies maintain no meaningful local presence and require a convenient venue to receive prospects. These preliminary evaluations may also transpire off campus at nearby employer offices, over the telephone, or potentially via the Internet. After wrapping up their initial screenings and paring down their candidate pools to those applicants that they wish to scrutinize further, employers then summon their top choices for further appraisal, which may shift off campus to company offices. Of course, employers ultimately award formal offers of full-time employment to those select individuals who sufficiently pass inspection and fully satisfy the company gatekeepers.

Interviewing on campus remains a prime job-search means for a host of reasons. First off, this principal instrument in your toolkit connects you with a respectable range of employers that you may not otherwise have access to. Unless the caliber of your graduating institution materially lags behind others, and the employment offerings within your campus career services center simply leave too much to be desired, mining for your future via these structured school-ground interviews advantageously registers your candidacy on the recruiting radars of top-shelf firms, obviously an acute edge over your outside-looking-in peers from the broader, employment-seeking populace. Students vying for first-rate employment opportunities external to the campus recruiting engine unquestionably face a more daunting path in drawing the attention of topflight firms. Unless you have personal connections or other opportune tie-ins, even irrespective of resume caliber, applicants who focus their efforts off campus typically must jump through greater hoops to bend the ears of sought-after employers, not to mention the markedly inferior hit rate in getting their resumes noticed in the first place. Perpetually deluged with torrents of resumes from eager-beaver graduating college seniors, top employers almost always pare down their recruiting grounds to only select universities, which effectively eliminates many hopefuls from consideration immediately.

Second, the general nature of the firms involved and the process itself certainly works in your favor. The campus-recruiting machine fosters circumstances conducive for graduating college seniors angling for their first full-time, professional position. Specifically, the sheer scale of the participating companies generally works to your advantage from a numbers perspective. The lion's share of companies converging upon your university to court fresh undergraduate recruits range from merely sizeable to industry-leading corporate giants, firms that inherently employ legions of full-time employees at any given time, particularly at the entry levels of the workforce. Here, company workforce deficiencies typically arise among the junior employee ranks with exceeding regularity, particularly within the numerous midsized and sizeable companies that systematically enlist significant quantities of fresh undergraduate recruits every year. Either by internal promotion or, in some instances, by outright defection from their first post-graduation employers, these new hires frequently maneuver through the corporate machinery in hasty fashion, which, of course, fosters the need for ongoing company feeding at the undergraduate recruitment trough. Therefore, your student status and the corresponding proximity to a campus career services center conceivably affords you access to a veritable bounty of frontline, entry-level employment opportunities. Over the course of my first full year of full-time employment after college, my titanic employer enlisted a whopping 175 fresh undergraduate recruits like myself into my particular corner of the firm. This fantastic figure excludes the multitudes of other fresh, post-college recruits drafted into numerous other areas of the company.

Additionally, the university recruiting engine aptly pairs candidate and opportunity. The campus-interviewing medium naturally links educated but inexperienced applicants—green aside from their prior involvement in get-your-feet-wet internships—with generic, nonspecialized but nonetheless frontline entry-level positions, as opposed to company roles that call for some measure of specific expertise and/or sector-relevant prior work experience. Given the scarcity of seasoning within new hires, these ground-level positions typically require only diligence and attention to detail at the outset, or at least until fresh recruits acquire valuable on-the-job experience. This harmonious marriage effectively expunges any risk of an ill fit between employer and new employee. Virtually every corporate suitor venturing to your university aims to recruit sound, dependable graduating college seniors for full-time employment—they maintain no designs of trekking to your campus in order to hire veteran workers in search of above-ground-level positions.

New entrants into the workforce garner the opportunity to dip their toes into the rapidly flowing corporate waters and accrue invaluable experience, while the employing contingent, on the other hand, reaps the benefits of dependable, affordable labor.

Furthermore, the firms participating in the process regularly enroll their new undergraduate hires into fruitful training programs. Extending anywhere from a condensed couple of weeks to an elongated couple of months or possibly longer, these offer refinement for incoming staff at the hands of versed instructors who mete out concise, intensive instruction amid a classroom setting, covering a full complement of topics pertinent to new recruit development. As a means of educating new hires on the nuances of their job duties and the dynamics of the company, in addition to easing newbies into the challenges they're likely to face in a fast-paced business, many employers typically slot their new hires into preparatory training sessions shortly after hiring, but prior to turning them loose within the uncompromising, professional battlefield. Certain companies prefer to enlist new recruits into their broader domains first and subsequently route them into their designated corners of the firm after training, whereas others hire directly into specific groups at the outset, granting individual department heads the power to effect their own hiring determinations.

When I started my first post-graduation job (but prior to being allocated into a particular group within the company), my new employer promptly directed me and a fresh crop of peers into the company's three-month training operation. Well regarded within the sector and particularly noted for its execution and depth, the touted program introduced us to an A-team of instructors and a cadre of other supporting crew members. In our case, this was a troupe of respected business school professors from distinguished academic programs in the New York area and several handpicked all-stars from the junior ranks of the company. The latter were exceedingly diligent young workers who had already established themselves as office standouts despite being only a year or two removed from their own college graduations. These ascending office favorites were generally brought in on an intermittent basis over the course of the training sessions to supply hands-on ministration and to shed light on the finer points of specific software-intensive tasks. The esteemed tutors from academia doled out concise but rich tutelage, encompassing a full palette of pertinent topics such as economics, accounting, banking, finance, and other essential subjects for new hires in my field. Moreover, this preparatory curriculum and hands-on learning exposed us to informative business school case study analyses, advanced computer-training workshops, simulated job-specific applications, and problem-solving exercises. The dynamic training regimen markedly bolstered my knowledge base and prepared me extensively for my specific full-time post and the awaiting corporate frontier.

Third, meeting with the blitz of firms venturing to your campus affords you immeasurable convenience. Relative to the prospect of ferrying all over town or out of town entirely to numerous geographic locales in sporadic, unpredictable fashion, auditioning for employment on your campus enables you to book a plentiful docket of early-round interviews with prominent employers within the cozy confines of your home turf within a tight, defined time frame.

For example, suppose you're eyeing a particular field after graduation and the relevant players in the space are slated to conduct their first-round screenings at your university during the first two weeks of December. Assuming you boast a competitive candidacy and elicit formal invitations to participate in a sizeable number of interviews, you might conceivably wrap up a good stretch of interviews in your own backyard and amid the early stages of your campaign—in this case, prior to breaking for the winter holidays.

Interviewing in such fashion blunts the risk of material interruption befalling your everyday routine. Again, in contrast to taking on an entirely inconvenient interviewing schedule, spinning the campus interviewing wheel with expedient campus interviewing allows you to more easily tend to your day-to-day undergraduate responsibilities, not only your academics but also any job-search opportunities outside of your campus career services center.

Of course, searching for full-time work outside the auspices of your university entails no such gravy train. Trekking to interviews in spotty fashion and to a potential cornucopia of off-campus destinations—not to mention the daunting task of lining up first-tier interviews entirely on your own—unquestionably presents a greater set of hurdles to surmount from a logistical standpoint. The off-campus process also demands more of your time, which can adversely impact your capacity to weave your senior-year interviewing schedule into your regular routine more seamlessly.

Amid my own ambitious path into the corporate realm, I temporarily recessed from my normal daily grind in order to pursue my employment Holy Grail full throttle. With my sights set on the shimmering lights and career promise of New York City, I stepped away from my daily routine, on three separate occasions no less, in order to venture to the East Coast and convene with a block of NYC employers atop my wish list. Although my travels to the Big Apple ultimately proved fruitful, and I successfully bagged my desired type of employment within my preferred geographic destination, needless to say, I reluctantly sacrificed attentiveness to my grade point average and postponed several interviewing opportunities in order to give full chase to my favored employment end game—a more accommodating flight path would surely have saved me a ton of time and headache.

Explore the offerings within your university career services center first and foremost. Rank this plan of attack at or very near the top of your job-search agenda because this avenue represents your best bet to connect with premium employers. Although the opportunities at your campus remain finite, given the straightforward, uncomplicated nature of the process, you will know where you stand—that is, after digging into this job-search channel, you will know whether or not you need to venture outside your university for further opportunities. For the majority of undergraduates, this approach will probably be the first and only resource required to connect with their future employers after graduation.

Networking

Scores of graduating college seniors find gainful post-graduation employment today via the profound power of networking. By commissioning individual connections—generally colleagues and acquaintances within the professional sphere—to refer resumes to higher-ups, hiring managers, and other company personnel, undergraduates regularly corral prime opportunities to interview and gain entry into premium bands of the business realm. Generally speaking, the caliber of employment you attain via networking remains otherwise out of reach without such deployment of your contacts. In other words, these opportunities may be outside the realm of possibilities if you stick to applying only via the traditional means of submitting your resume to human resources and engaging in subsequent telephone follow-up just like any other candidates from the general talent pool.

Networking remains a prime job-search strategy by virtue of its capacity to mutually benefit both the employer and the recruit. On the one hand, in securing third-party referrals that net interviewing opportunities, undergraduates draw premium corporate attention and ultimately consideration from their favored employers that they may not necessarily experience when applying via traditional means. More precisely, they avoid going unnoticed by firms or having their resumes get lost in the shuffle among the tides of resumes already flowing unrelentingly into the offices of top-shelf employers. Particularly among the upper tier of the corporate food chain, businesses harbor precious little time to pore over the resumes of each and every individual tendering an application and, as a result, consistently scrutinize incoming resume submissions from the broader candidate reservoir in only cursory fashion, if at all. All too often, resumes are dismissed and ultimately deposited into electronic or paper file wastelands, never to be seen or heard from again.

On the other side of the coin, by bringing fit new enlistments into the fold via such means, businesses mitigate recruiting risk. They downgrade their odds of adding fresh hires who ultimately fall short, if not well short, of expectations within the workplace. Given the acute incentive for referrers to convey only first-rate prospects up the corporate ladder, their employers in effect reap introduction to only sound, pre-screened candidates that comfortably surpass or at least perform in line with company forecasts when all is said and done. Such practice surely translates into greater conviction in their decision making for new personnel and produces a corresponding superior hit rate relative to hiring unknown candidates from outside the firm.

Firms face recruiting hazards each and every time they draft unfamiliar prospects into their domains. Despite the general presence of sound company-screening procedures for new personnel, a smattering of employment hopefuls present themselves commendably on paper and interview effectively in person, only to underperform upon assuming their new full-time posts, hanging their new employers out to dry. Of course, businesses cannot entirely insulate themselves from the risks of feeding at the undergraduate trough, nor can they implement infallible filtration measures that faultlessly weed out every subpar prospective recruit that arrives to interview. Employers maintain no surefire means of forecasting the workplace dexterity of the new recruits they reel in from outside the firm, but through referrals, they can possess ample firsthand information on the finesse of internal candidates.

Furthermore, hiring new personnel in such fashion unquestionably fosters greater efficiency for employers. In utilizing this uncomplicated recruiting vehicle, employers avert ensnarement within an otherwise arduous screening process and successfully restock their entry-level ranks with qualified new graduates. In effect, these third-party mentions take the place of preliminary interviewing rounds, which expedites the paths of fresh workforce blood into the full-time labor force. Candidates may even bypass initial screening layers altogether and sit down directly with senior personnel or other top-ranking company decision makers at the outset.

Of course, in the absence of hiring via trusted referral, employers inevitably confront the daunting task of gauging fresh applicant aptitude from scratch. Employers must suffer through the conventional, toilsome, resource-consuming (and of course, not always fail-safe) applicant filtration procedures in order to connect with capable talent and fulfill their entry-level personnel needs. Obviously, such practice soaks up finite company manpower, diverting it toward the corporate recruiting engine and away from core business execution. The more time employees devote to recruiting, the less time that remains for routine office business. Employees involved in the candidate-evaluation mechanism must break away from their regular workplace duties in order to support the broader company-recruiting process.

Even with sound corporate screening practices in place, flawed entry-level hirelings nevertheless slip through the corporate cracks. Especially among the more sizeable entities that employ scores of full-time personnel at any given time and manage large-scale recruiting operations, employers occasionally fumble when appraising new prospects and get stuck with less-than-ideal recruits. Despite appearances on paper, recruits drafted outside the firm remain unknown commodities and forecasting the workplace skills of such applicants simply remains an inexact science. Further, superior resumes do not always spell first-rate office performance, as any employer will surely attest. Unquestionably, employers favor safe bets over unknown, risky propositions and prefer to recruit candidates with whom they maintain some degree of confidence and familiarity.

I personally witnessed such recruiting busts shortly after signing on with my first post-college employer. Over the course of only two years of corporate servitude—I exited the firm after that and plied my trade elsewhere, as was common practice for pre-business school analysts in my position—I encountered shoddy office execution on occasion at the hands of co-workers recruited directly out of school. Despite the implementation of effective examination procedures for newfangled recruits, much to my dismay, I crossed paths with company peers during that brief two-year stretch whose workplace aptitude certifiably lagged behind their credentials on paper. One in particular had even earned his bachelor's degree from a top-notch program within the Boston-area mecca of elite academic institutions; the revelation of his exemplary university pedigree left me utterly dumbfounded after having witnessed his blatant office failure firsthand. Although representative of only a miniscule slice of the broader frontline staff, these office warts had somehow managed to slip past the firm's stout recruiting defenses and effectively hoodwinked their way into enviable positions.

Adding insult to injury, my employer abstained from upsetting the apple cart, seldom tendering these office stinkers their well-deserved walking papers. Such guarded practice from the decision makers within the firm inevitably gave rise to a thorny situation in the office trenches. After firmly establishing their incompetence, these disappointing slackers were routinely passed over for new work assignments and simply languished on the company payroll—which undoubtedly fostered deep resentment among the already overworked office core—until finally making out the writing on the wall and eventually unloading their underwhelming talents onto other unsuspecting employers.

Why retain such bottlenecks in the workforce? Either to save face—severing ties with new hires with any measure of regularity surely reflects poorly on businesses—or for legal rationales in today's politically correct, lawsuit-fraught business climate, employers regularly refrain from simply cutting bait when confronted with such issues. Unfortunately, their risk aversion and obstinate adherence to the status quo—stubbornly holding off on rocking the boat and retaining visibly dead weight on the company roster—however maddening for the regular frontline staff, minimizes the damage done. It offers employers the path of least resistance and lowest risk relative to the prospect, however slight, of shameless and frivolous but potentially harmful legal action from maligned, recently dismissed employees. Obviously, employers prefer to avoid such entanglements.

Look at networking from the employer's perspective. Suppose, for example, you hold down a senior-level post at a top-end employer and suddenly find yourself in a bind. A productive junior-level recruit abruptly announces his intentions to leave the company, much to your surprise, turning in his two weeks' notice and leaving you high and dry. Operating in a hyper-competitive, niche market with a modest, streamlined crew, you can ill afford the sudden reduction in your numbers, even if only by one at the entry-level ranks. You need to come up with a sensible remedy fast. Upon catching wind of the wave-making announcement, one of your most dependable young workers steps forward with a possible solution. Aware of the hole on the front lines of the workforce and the need for a quick, reliable fix, he tells you of a prime candidate, in his view, to fill the recently vacated post. An astute peer from school, he explains, is in the market for a new job. Currently employed in a comparable capacity at a competing firm but not necessarily wedded to his employer long term, he has expressed an interest in bringing his talents over to your first-rate employer. Looking for an upgrade, he would jump at the chance to interview for the newly opened position. Industrious and well regarded, he has received nothing but high praise and exaltation from his bosses, as outlined in his most recent performance review, according to your devoted subordinate. Anticipating considerable interest from you, your trusted deputy offers to retrieve a copy of his colleague's resume for your review.

How do you respond? How do you react to the proposal offered up by your loyal office follower? Of course, you give his idea strong consideration. Given the alternative of posting an employment listing, filtering through an inordinate number of resume submissions, and then suffering through the painstaking matter of interviewing hopefuls by the truckload in search of a match—effectively starting from scratch—and even then there are no guarantees, surely you receive his overture with open arms. Surely you fully entertain the idea of taking a long, hard look at this seemingly exemplary prospect rather than dive headfirst into a taxing, drawn-out recruiting predicament that pulls you away from your regular workplace duties. Already versed in the sector and up to speed on the demands of the position given his current footing in the industry, and apparently chomping at the bit to come on board with your employer, this proven commodity may be just what the doctor ordered. Given the seemingly great fit, he may very well hit the ground running and fill the void left by your ex-employee. Assuming he lives up to the hype and assimilates seamlessly, bringing in this promising prospective addition to the payroll solves your issue in one fell swoop, saving you a ton of time and hassle and sparing you from the headache of a tedious, time-consuming search for a replacement. Such a move permits you to maintain focus on your regular workplace duties and waste zero time sorting through the sea of wild cards from the outside. Having a reliable voice vouch for his skill set makes all the difference.

In order to network effectively and gain introduction to top-shelf employers, exploit the full range of your connections. Capitalize on your family ties, both immediate and extended, and also on your personal relationships with friends, acquaintances, and other known figures who might be able to help. Invoke a "numbers game" approach, and thoroughly implore your network of kin and colleagues to pass your resume along to higher-ups, hiring managers, other apt parties, and even elsewhere, such as to contacts of your contacts who may in turn endorse your candidacy to their immediate superiors or potentially refer you to other relevant parties.

That is not to say you should indiscriminately lobby every living member of your family tree presently holding down serviceable employment and fervently seek out every acquaintance or prospective connection that has crossed your path in recent years. Rather, implement a sweeping, shrewd plan of attack in which you leave no stone unturned and resourcefully canvass each and every pertinent colleague and acquaintance you have to assist in your job-search efforts.

Tap into your top options above all else, of course, but also give attention to your second-tier resources. In other words, don't entirely neglect or dissuade yourself from investigating any potential allies for your campaign that, although seemingly of only scant relevance in terms of their capacity to refer your resume, may yet prove instrumental. Unless they bear absolutely no value whatsoever to your efforts, reach out and initiate communication, in any event. You certainly have nothing to lose.

For example, suppose a successful aunt maintains a senior, front-office post with a distinguished local business, and, aware of your grand designs to find a job with a premium-tier employer, she generously volunteers to rustle up a top-shelf interviewing opportunity for you within her company. Unfortunately, however, you maintain only sparse interest in landing a full-time gig with her employer. As another example, suppose you firmly desire a position with a close colleague's respected employer, but after approaching the firm and exploring your possibilities there, you discover that the firm has recently instituted a seemingly inflexible company-wide hiring freeze. Lastly, suppose you recently completed a productive undergraduate internship with a prominent industry player in your preferred sector. You met expectations and meshed exceedingly well with your office mates, bonding particularly well with your chief internship coordinator, a highly regarded company employee. However, despite your first-rate workplace performance and smooth assimilation into the challenging business environment, you emerged without an offer of full-time employment and without any assurances that the company might be willing to retain your services on a full-time basis after graduation.

Even though your prospects to obtain entry into any of these firms appear virtually nil, reach out to each of the individuals within these hypothetical examples, in any event. Don't prematurely judge their ability to further your campaign, and don't immediately bump them from your contact list just yet, as a number of your peers may misguidedly do. Telephone each of them, even in the face of long odds or seeming incompatibility with your ambitions. At the end of the day, until you reach out to them, you cannot definitively ascertain their potential to maneuver on your behalf.

Perhaps your go-getter aunt may surprise you with an intriguing ground-level post with her employer previously unknown to you. Maybe the seemingly impossible hiring moratorium described in the second scenario may ultimately prove temporary or even penetrable through other means. In the third instance, perhaps your pleasant apprenticeship supervisor may offer to pull a few strings on your behalf and carve out a spot for you within the full-time company roster, even if upper management previously harbored no designs of inviting you to return to the firm after you wrap up your schooling. Despite the professed lack of evident or appealing opportunity and the seemingly insurmountable obstacles within each of these situations, your chances of connecting with a legitimate opportunity surely exceed zero—although improbable, these scenarios could actually result in worthwhile employment. You certainly have nothing to lose.

After disseminating copies of my resume to distinguished East Coast firms on my post-graduation radar, I received a dismissive company form letter from one firm informing me of its decision to decline my bid for full-time employment. When I received the deflating rejection letter, I immediately reached out to a personal ally within the firm, a respected post-MBA company contributor. Despite the apparent death knell to my possibilities with the company, I diplomatically implored him to nudge his superiors on my behalf and revisit the company's prior ruling on my application. Not long after deploying my inside man—voilá!—I received word from the firm of their prior oversight in reviewing my resume. After a dose of crafty maneuvering by my insider, the hiring powers effectively reversed course and rescinded their prior dismissal, even though my candidacy, of course, had remained entirely unchanged since my initial submission. As I touched on earlier, given the volumes of resumes incessantly streaming into the company's center of operations, human resources, in all likelihood, offered up only scant attention to my resume in the first place, ultimately chucking it into the sea of forgotten resumes from the plethora of graduating college seniors presently taking up hard drive and filing cabinet space within the company's back offices.

The bottom line is to utilize your full sweep of familiar connections, even in instances with perceptibly lean prospects for employment opportunities. Refrain from striking any such individuals from your contact list, and resourcefully petition them. Ultimately, they may link you with a fruitful post-graduation job, even if, on the surface, these prospective connections offer minimal or no value to your campaign.

Moreover, call on any and all potential agents for your campaign because they may very well refer you indirectly to real opportunities elsewhere. Even if immediate opportunities within their employers remain an ill fit with your career objectives or simply appear unattainable, certain contacts possess the potential to tap into their own contact lists on your behalf and route you accordingly to other connections who may in turn facilitate your employment with another firm entirely. At the end of the day, the true value of your contacts extends beyond their immediate capacity to endorse your candidacy within their employers and lies with their potential to link you, directly or indirectly, with opportunities on par with your personal standard.

This is exactly how I landed my first big-league gig after college. While sorting through my best leads during my senior year, I contacted a business school colleague of a primary personal contact, a first-string contributor within one of the sought-after firms on my wish list. By this point, I had, of course, also set in motion the process of lining up interviews with my primary connection's employer. After talking with me over the telephone and finally meeting with me in person a couple of times—primarily to size me up firsthand prior to pulling any strings on my behalf—my newfound connection eventually agreed to hand my resume to the appropriate parties with his employer, which all but ensured my landing an interview with the esteemed firm. Eventually, after successfully squaring off with a mountain of quality interviewing competition and satisfying the full sequence of exacting company interviewers at all stages of the interviewing conveyor belt, I triumphantly earned a spot with a sought-after professional enterprise.

Next, in keeping with a comprehensive plan of attack, mine for value within the lower bands of your contact hierarchy. Akin to the above, don't prejudge or reach any definitive conclusions regarding the relevance or effectiveness of these lesser resources in terms of their capacity to materially aid your cause. Never completely discount any potential for merit within these lowest tiers of your known resources. In the interest of covering all your bases, resourcefully lob probing telephone calls, particularly after exhausting your best bets, or if you simply remain out of other viable options with certain tier-one employers on your radar.

As an example, suppose you really want a position with a particular esteemed employer, but after having contacted the firm on multiple occasions and having your overtures go repeatedly rebuffed or ignored, you appear all but out of options with this individual company. You maintain a connection there of sorts, but only of the very marginal variety, in the form of a long-tenured, executive administrative assistant with whom you have a common acquaintance. Although undoubtedly a long shot to refer your resume to any top-ranking figures within the firm, given her conspicuous standing on the other side of the invisible but distinctly demarcated office partition dividing the frontline office citizens from the subordinate rank and file workers, telephone her anyway. Given your complete lack of alternatives with this particular employer, overlook her second-fiddle professional stature and her presumably slim influence within the firm, and approach her for assistance nevertheless. Perhaps she performs her daily duties without a hitch and without complaint and, as a result, maintains a rock-solid professional rapport with her immediate boss, to the extent that he may conceivably lend an ear if she were to offer up a legitimate referral. Perhaps she also earns a sufficient measure of respect from her officemates and, as a result, maintains her status as a critical component of the team and may therefore pass your resume up the company chain of command.

Take advantage of your full sweep of contacts, including your lowest-tier connections, but respect the hierarchy of your resources. Power-rank them in descending order of importance with respect to their utility and relevance to your campaign, and then canvass accordingly. Solicit your most propitious contacts first and foremost, of course, and then simply make your way down the list.

Consider the following example. Suppose you covet entry into a hot field. You kick off your job search and dispense copies of your resume to each of the relevant, in-demand employers in the space. Aware of the game-changing benefits of having an inside connection to maneuver on your behalf, you ask your mentor and main contacts for any ties to the sector. After making the rounds with your principal resources, you come up with three separate individuals: a successful older cousin entrenched in a great career at a distinguished industry leader; a diligent colleague from your university a year your senior who translated his undergraduate deeds into a respectable, frontline post at an accomplished, mid-sized enterprise; and, lastly, a mid-level employee at a commendable, modest outfit who, although productive, earns his paychecks in the company operations department, obviously a less-heralded area of the firm and outside of your preferred space.

Of course, reach out to your established elder cousin first and foremost. She clearly represents your best bet of the three to pull off a consequential referral. Surely her sway within her esteemed employer capacitates her to pull a few strings on your behalf and get your foot in the door to interview. Given her presumably expansive contact list, she may even route you elsewhere in the event you come up empty with her employer. Second, call up your schoolmate from a year ago. Although green and not yet a consequential company decision maker, this investigable resource still carries enough clout to put in a good word and get your resume in front of the right people, given his front-row position. During my own hunt for employment, my best contacts simply placed phone calls to their human resources departments or, specifically, to the central figures in those offices, and that was generally enough to do the trick. Lastly, telephone the mid-range wage earner from the company operations division. Although a second-tier resource at best, given his non-upper-level position in a necessary but ultimately supportive, non-revenue-generating group, telephone him, in any event. Ring him up, despite the fact that your chances of landing a top-tier opportunity as a result of his jockeying seem like a long shot. See if he has any tricks up his sleeve at all, particularly if he represents your sole link to this particular employer and the alternative consists of submitting an application and then hoping and praying for a call back, akin to the mass of undergraduate employment hopefuls from the broader candidate pool. You never know. Like the example involving the administrative assistant above, perhaps he may accommodate your plight after all. Perhaps he may recruit a heavy hitter from your targeted corner of the company to work some magic. Perhaps he may place a call to a receptive higher-up or a human resources staff member and find a way to accommodate your request for an interview. Let me say it again: You have nothing to lose.

Pursue any and all potentially viable paths to gainful employment by way of your connections, no matter how slim the chances of your unearthing a diamond in the rough. Going the extra mile and prying into every nook and cranny unquestionably exceeds applying yourself only moderately or limiting yourself to only your best bets. Turn your contact list inside out to squeeze every drop from the reservoir of options at your disposal. At the end of the day, this approach will maximize your prospects to uncover a hidden gem within your personal contacts and ultimately connect you with the job you most desire.

In addition to exploring the full range of your existing contacts, also forge novel connections. Expand your networking radius beyond your immediate circle of relatives, friends, acquaintances, and other familiar faces, and scout fresh means of acquainting yourself with prime new allies for your campaign. Branch out from your family and your personal ties with colleagues, and beef up your contact list. Explore any number of avenues to cultivate newfangled relationships with fruitful resources within the professional sphere who might further your crusade and route you to gainful full-time employment.

First and foremost, exploit your commonalities with others. In order to bend the ears of fresh allies with whom you maintain no prior familiarity and conceivably recruit them to operate on your behalf, scour the white-collar grid for helpful figures, ideally those employed in first-tier capacities within the businesses you're interested in. Seek out those with whom you have a common thread, who, by virtue of that connection and with a major contribution from your evident initiative, may prove receptive and refer your resume up the chain of command within their employers. As I have previously advanced, they might even route you to contacts at other companies, who may then recommend your candidacy as well.

Specifically, cash in on your alumni network. Scour the Internet, probe your campus career services center, and also approach current connections and potentially your fellow graduating seniors for the names of any relevant graduates from prior years presently holding down full-time roles within your targeted sector.

If applicable, comb your campus for a university "buddy list" or an unofficial alumni directory containing up-to-date contact and employer information of former students who presently hold first-string jobs within your favored corner of the corporate marketplace. Of course, the caliber of these information stores varies from one to the next, largely depending upon underlying university caliber— i.e., certain "buddy lists" comprise superior content and depth and render immense utility, whereas others contain only meager information, if much at all. Sometimes, less-heralded institutions devoid of an operative alumni network may yield only a directory with scant information several notches below what you had hoped for. Furthermore, some of these organized records are readily accessible and easy to locate online or floating around your campus in some form or fashion, while others are kept under lock and key and maintained in virtual secrecy, making them much more difficult to procure. In certain instances, your university may effectively sanction the upkeep and dissemination of such data. For example, a prominent campus organization, with approval from its constituents, might systematically compile and publish relevant personal information about members who currently hold productive professional positions.

In lieu of your unearthing any such information gold mines on your university grounds, assemble your own such file via your own resourceful legwork.

Additionally, capitalize on your involvement in group activities. Take advantage of your association with organized clubs and activities both on and off campus that, as a byproduct of membership, connects you to professionals who may conceivably lend a helping hand. In particular, exploit your affiliation with campus fraternities or sororities, organized athletic endeavors, academic/honors societies, major-specific guilds, international student organizations, student government, charitable ventures, armed services, and virtually any other constructive outlets that foster a palpable measure of fellowship among their members. Translate any such interests into meaningful conversations with individuals who are in a position to refer your resume or introduce you to appealing employment opportunities. You may well encounter people with more than one area of overlap. For example, you may be introduced to an elder alumnus or alumna with a distinguished career who also was a member of your campus fraternity. In this instance, you reel in a weighty backer for your candidacy via a robust, doubly reinforced kinship.

Of course, be selective with the affiliations you farm. That is, tap into only those memberships that you may realistically extract any juice from—draw from those associations that both cultivate a concrete sense of camaraderie across their ranks and also encompass a sufficient measure of top-shelf constituents. As an example, capitalize on your affiliation with a university sorority or fraternity. Close-knit social fraternal orders almost always breed an acute sense of sisterhood or brotherhood among their initiates and frequently entail ample reach, to the extent that you may successfully uncover and connect with consequential working professionals more than eager to assist you in any way they can.

Accordingly, skip over any communal associations that offer virtually no opportunities for networking in this sense. Don't waste your efforts on enterprises that, although worthy of your time and worthy of reference on your resume, ultimately offer only meager or no legitimate chances to gain access to fellow members in the professional world.

For example, consider membership in Golden Key International Honor Society. Although worth the price of admission for most students and generally well received by company gatekeepers, acceptance into GKIHS, unfortunately, holds only nominal value in terms of the fraternity it propagates among its alumni members. The networking opportunities it affords are minimal, excluding any personal relationships you cultivate with fellow members during your participation in GKIHS events. Despite its advantages for resume and other purposes (e.g., scholarships and internships), at the end of the day, Golden Key—billed as the world's largest collegiate honor society, with over two million members strong and with widespread reach that spans international borders—simply remains too widespread and impersonal for you to realistically leverage membership into relationships with previously unfamiliar parties within the professional sphere.

Next, exploit your geographic origins. In the event you rightfully claim membership in a particular minority group or class of people on the basis of territorial or cultural roots, capitalize on this identifiable marker. Tap into any such distinguishable identifiers, and leverage them into viable resources. For example, if you or your forebears emigrated from another nation, then certainly take advantage of the connection you have with others of the same ethnicity. Reach out to the pertinent professionals bearing your same heritage, and ask them to facilitate your campaign.

Although perhaps most applicable for international students, domestic graduating college seniors may also have a finger in the pie—opportunities to capitalize on geographic ties are not necessarily confined only to non-domestic-born job seekers. In certain instances, native-born undergraduate employment hopefuls may also translate their hometown connections into favorable contacts. They may encounter instances in which their upbringing proves advantageous.

I encountered such a scenario during my own journey into the post-graduation frontier. After returning from a trying week-long trek to New York City amid the latter half of my senior year, where I met with prospective employers and embarked upon a string of informational interviews, I successfully wrested a coveted invitation to participate in a full-day's worth of final-round screenings with one of the companies I had previously met with. Prior to my final return trip to vie for an offer with this particular employer, I received a call from a colleague within the company who had previously referred my resume and helped land me an initial interview with the firm in the first place. He called to inform me that, as it turned out, I had already rubbed elbows with one of the interviewers slated to participate in the forthcoming undergraduate interviewing judgment day. During my first swim through the building for first-round interviews, my inside man had introduced me to a forefront company professional from my home city who had also attended college at a prominent institution very near my alma mater. I recalled that during that initial encounter, we had chatted cordially about our common city and also, of course, touched on my current courtship with his employer. Cordial and approachable, my fellow hometown native proved very receptive to my plight at that first encounter, generously offering up his business card on my way out the door. Now, upon hearing this acutely promising news, I immediately reached out to this newfound connection and proceeded to update him on my current interviewing status with the company—specifically, my acceptance into the upcoming, all-important, final-round interviewing sessions. Pleased to hear of my success in making it this far, he applauded my progress and, most importantly, confirmed his firsthand involvement in the imminent interviews. Furthermore, much to my elation and pleasant surprise, he also conveyed his firm, personal commitment to my candidacy. Assuming I turned in a convincing interviewing performance with his fellow screeners, he basically pledged to go to bat for me within the post-interview war room where the interviewing panel collectively sorted through their opinions and ultimately handed down their final verdicts on the employment fates of each of the interviewees.

Even though I ultimately accepted an offer of employment elsewhere, my particular geographic ties in this instance bolstered my odds with this potential employer markedly. Although I wielded a competitive candidacy and had already survived the first round of cuts prior to my falling into the timely introduction, my origins unexpectedly netted me a critical "in" with a key in-house supporter. This not only distinguished me from the balance of the broader candidate pool but also pegged me as much more of a known commodity, unquestionably an appreciable edge over the remaining interviewing competition. Without the fortuitous intersection with the ranking company figure and major contributor to the final round interviewing proceedings, I surely would have remained on equal footing with the other hopefuls still in the mix.

Milk your common threads because people invariably favor others with whom they find something in common. That is, individuals in position to carry out an endorsement undoubtedly remain far more prone to "take care of their own" and throw their weight behind candidates whom they identify with or with whom they have a perceived measure of fraternity or association.

Moreover, the presence of material overlapping spheres provides the necessary grounds for reaching out to prospective connections in the first place. These tie-ins to others effectively bridge the chasm between yourself, an unseasoned unknown, and the experienced white-collar recipients of your overtures who already have plenty of obligations and responsibilities on their plates. In short, these commonalities enable you to initially connect with desirable corporate allies. Approaching unfamiliar figures within the professional sphere without any legitimate common knots is simply not feasible; you cannot just pick up the telephone and dial unfamiliar professionals at potential employers out of the blue and realistically expect them to receive your advances favorably, let alone offer up their assistance.

Second, explore the use of social media. Hop aboard the growing virtual community and networking train, and ride it on your journey toward post-graduation employment. In order to get the most out of this approach and facilitate your introduction to timely facilitators of your campaign, plug into the information superhighway and traverse the full panorama of relevant players in the space. Fully exploit each of the relevant Internet-based outfits that maintains a meaningful share of the broader social media pie and that also offers a platform conducive for professional networking, as opposed to sites playing host to casual or nonprofessional traffic. These sources might facilitate connections with company hiring managers and other professionals in the corporate world. Some of these sites also allow you to apply directly for jobs with select employers.

To get started, sign up with each of the obvious players, such as LinkedIn, Facebook, Google+, Twitter, plus any other notable up-and-comers that may have popped up and gained a foothold in the past five minutes. Next, craft a concise, unblemished profile for each of the vehicles you join, or tidy up those already in use. Include your relevant personal information, tailor your profile to your particular career objectives, and consider adding a personal branding statement. Of course, be sure to eliminate any unsavory or loose content that casts you in any manner in an unprofessional light and potentially compromises your appeal in the eyes of potential suitors. For example, expletive-laden commentary or questionable pictures of yourself amid a festive backdrop replete with alcoholic beverage in hand uploaded onto a popular social networking site are not in your best interest. Particularly among distinguished, white-collar circles, employers and recruiters avoid needless risk and thoroughly background-check all of the candidates who pass their initial screening, whom they wish to bring back for further review. Employers meticulously comb over personal social media pages plus any other manifestations of your online presence. Where applicable, consider retaining a fee-based, third-party service to effectively sanitize your presence within social networking platforms, and anywhere else within the virtual world for that matter, prior to your reaching out to any tier-one employers.

After registering and artfully molding concise personal bios for each of your social media accounts, effect any number of measures you can take to bolster your connectivity and build your network. First off, transition any existing social contacts into professional contacts wherever applicable. Next, echoing a familiar theme, employ a numbers game approach, and link directly with sought-after employers aplenty. Moreover, using an instant messenger as a prime means of communication—at least until you gain relevant contact information—reach out and connect virtually with company hiring managers or other relevant human resources staff, as well as novel prospective contacts. Lastly, join and actively participate in groups and group discussions. Engage in any and all activities that fan out your cyber tentacles, bolster your networking reach, and connect you with helpful professionals. Broadcast your candidacy to the widest possible audience within cyberspace. At the end of the day, employers, professionals, and headhunters all utilize social media, so, of course, you need to use it, too.

Third, embark on campus-recruiting functions. Within these affairs, gainfully employed alumni from select firms typically venture to your university on a casual basis, often under the context of a social mixer or other type of relaxed event, at varying points during the year. The company representatives making the trip aim to market their employers to sought-after undergraduates and to aid in the recruitment of blue-chip, ground-level candidates for open positions. Attend any and all such events involving companies on your radar. In addition to utilizing them as a means of upgrading your comfort level with corporate professionals as I described in chapter 1, also exploit the opportunity to network and forge newfound connections. Actively engage your event hosts, involve yourself in any relevant discussions, and, if not already volunteered by session's end, request the business cards and contact information of the company representatives putting on the gatherings.

Often, these alumni will identify with you as a former student, which can make the process easier. On the whole, these individuals are more than happy to aid ambitious graduating college seniors aiming to break into their fields. They may very well willingly hand over their telephone numbers and e-mail addresses to those who convey a positive interest in their sectors or companies and, of course, who present themselves well in person.

Lastly, attend job fairs and other industry events. In addition to scouting career fairs on and off campus as I touched on previously, frequent conferences and any other relevant goings-on within your targeted sector that may connect you with helpful working professionals from companies of interest. Just as with on-campus networking events with successful alumni, wade into such endeavors and interact in a fearless manner with company representatives: offer up pertinent inquiries, hand out numerous copies of your resume, collect business cards or other contact information, and potentially even apply for jobs on the spot when appropriate. However, proceed with caution, particularly when dealing with any off-campus employment bazaars. Steer clear of any low-grade, dime-a-dozen assemblies seemingly open to anyone and for the most part offering acquaintance with only unappetizing back office, commission-based sales, or other flatly inferior positions devoid of any long-range opportunity for you.

As you solicit potential facilitators for your campaign, be sure to do so in a seemly manner. Convey your ambition and your preparedness for the professional frontier, but also blanket your appeals within a humble, courteous air that triggers an optimal response and implants a decisively favorable impression with the individuals you petition, both known and unknown alike. Certainly refrain from approaching people in any manner of a presumptive drift—i.e., that you *expect* any recipients of your overtures to automatically come to your aid and promptly pair you with five-star employment. Even when approaching relatives and individuals with whom you maintain a prior relationship, with the slight exception of immediate family or very close colleagues who already know you all too well and require no such mindful diplomacy, do not assume that because you know them well or because you share the same family tree, they will spontaneously drop everything on their plates in order to tend to your needs. After all, you are effectively requesting that they step back from their regular routines and lay their credibility on the line to a degree in order to give attention to your career ambitions. Seasoned professionals surely have more important items to tend to over the resume-referral needs of eager undergraduates.

Tread in such fashion because virtually all of the individuals you approach remain far more apt to support hopefuls who reach out with an earnest, respectful tone. Irrespective of the professional stature of these prospective contacts or your level of familiarity with them, such individuals by and large favor applicants who not only boast superior initiative and smashing candidacies on paper but who also exhibit first-rate poise. The working professionals on the receiving end of your advances already maintain agendas chock-full of pressing daily tasks and responsibilities at any given time and therefore harbor precious little patience for young, cocky aspirants who approach in anything less than a civil, unassuming vein.

Experienced professionals from the competitive working world are undoubtedly opposed to endorsing any employment hopefuls whom they perceive as arrogant or who simply fail to sufficiently impress in person with respect to their personal demeanor. Irrespective of applicant caliber, potential resume sponsors harbor meager or entirely no inclination to offer their assistance to undergraduates who come across as anything short of self-starting or who give off the impression that they only seek to secure a handout. This pertains to individuals who seemingly have their arms wrapped around their operations only half-heartedly and approach as though they expect their enlisted messengers to effect the bulk of the heavy lifting on their behalf and deliver them prime post-graduation opportunities on a silver platter. The worst offenders typically squeeze their contacts for a recommendation only to promptly disappear, never to be seen or heard from again barring their eventual recruitment into the company in question. Working professionals shy away from lending assistance to job seekers who give off the impression that they maintain only scant interest in helping themselves first and foremost. Those who might refer you to their superiors prefer to aid ambitious candidates who fervently convey their ambition and willingness to do everything in their power to punch their ticket into a premium-tier job but simply need a helping hand in getting their feet through the door.

Pursue informational interviews. When reaching out for the first time to prospective allies to your campaign, introduce yourself, reference your common threads where applicable, and communicate your rationale for calling—that is, your impending graduation and corresponding mission to break into the corporate world in worthwhile fashion. Telegraph your interest in your petitioned party's sector, but rather than impatiently jump the gun and immediately press for a referral (and risk driving away potentially instrumental individuals in the process), employ a subtle approach and request that they sit down with you face-to-face for an informational interviewing session.

While these may not be official interviews per se—you are certainly not interviewing for a specific full-time post—informational interviews, in addition to rendering an excellent means of upgrading your level of interaction with industry professionals, also afford you a prime mode of retrieving helpful insight and counsel from experienced voices from the corporate world against an informal, unassuming backdrop. Take full advantage of these opportunities to acquire perspective, and pick the brains of the seasoned professionals at your disposal. Despite the laid-back nature of these one-on-ones, research your hosts' employers ahead of time, arrive with extra copies of your resume, and wear the appropriate dress—err on the side of caution and overdress as opposed to underdress, as a general rule of thumb. Furthermore, transmit an aura of quiet confidence and professionalism, and offer up astute questions for your interviewer such as: How should I differentiate myself within my formal interviews? What is to be expected of me during my first year on the job? What does a typical day in the office entail? What industry trends does your host foresee on the horizon? How does your host's employer fit into the broader picture within the sector?

Perhaps most importantly, informational interviews enable you to potentially shed the "prospective" qualifier from the prospective corporate contacts you approach. Although these meetings more or less transpire under the informal pretense of your personal education and growth as a candidate, consulting like this with veteran professionals in your field, assuming all goes well, allows you to spin previously unknown white-collar names from your prospective contact list into actual allies for your campaign. Such compatriots hopefully will go to bat for you with their employers and potentially even elsewhere, depending upon your circumstances.

That is not to say you should engage in any manner of deceptive practice. Rather, proceed opportunistically, and be prepared to pounce on any chance to reel in new contacts and translate them into legitimate resources for your operation.

In sum, informational interviews provide you with colorful industry perspective, confidence-bolstering connectivity with seasoned corporate operatives and, perhaps most critically, the opportunity to showcase your abilities to individuals in position to help you in your job-search efforts. Your informational interviewing hosts, although they may not necessarily set out with such designs in mind, may ultimately elect to throw their weight behind your candidacy to their employers, or possibly elsewhere, as an advantageous by-product. Akin to other professionals you consult, informational interviewers, seeing you as a younger version of themselves, are often more than happy to aid ambitious graduating college seniors who project themselves well in person and convey sincere interest in breaking into their chosen fields.

Although persistence is almost always key for attaining optimal results and getting the most out of informational interviewing, you conceivably do not need to lift a finger in order to corral such allies into your corner. Assuming you carry yourself well and boast a competitive resume, your interviewers may pledge their support largely unprompted. After sizing up your resume and your personal presentation over the telephone or in person, many professionals may offer to "see what they can do" and pass along your resume within their employing offices and within their own contact circles, prior to you even requesting such assistance.

In other instances, the solicited parties may even offer to refer your resume without the conventional face-to-face formality entirely. In full appreciation of your drive and core motivation after digesting your resume and hearing your initial pitch over the telephone, these individuals may simply cut to the chase and propose that, in the interest of time, you bypass the customary in-person meeting altogether, particularly if they can just as easily lend their assistance and respond to your questions over the telephone or via e-mail. This is a much more commonplace outcome when dealing with individuals with whom you maintain a degree of familiarity or an existing relationship, someone who already knows you and has faith in your credentials. Already confident in your skill set and your ability to thrive within the formal interrogation pressure cooker, they may pledge an open line of communication with you, volunteer to hand your resume up the chain of command, and tap their connections on your behalf without having met with you face-to-face. Still, if you prefer one-on-one meetings, they will presumably comply with your wishes and sit down with you in person. The majority of the parties you approach will be more inclined to adhere to the standard protocol and engage you in person prior to their referring your resume anywhere.

If your interviewing hosts fail to offer to pass along your resume, broach the topic of them referring your resume prior to leaving the face-to-face meeting. Drop subtle hints, in the appropriate tone, regarding your acute interest in employment within your petitioned party's sector. If all else fails, get down to brass tacks and inquire outright about the existence of any entry-level employment opportunities within your hosts' employers. At this stage, they should certainly realize that you would gladly welcome a referral.

I embarked upon a number of these fruitful powwows amid my own senior-year march into the corporate frontier. Aiming to amass as much third-party input and counsel prior to taking on my top-drawer interviews and to milk as many referrals as possible along the way, I diplomatically requested each of the relevant connections on my list to sit down with me for an informational interview. As a result of my presentation and initiative, I evoked a largely positive response. In addition, I netted pertinent field and job-specific enlightenment that increased my interviewing aptitude and knowledge base, such as insight into broader industry trends and into the principal players and other ranking entities jockeying for position in the larger sector. Most importantly, informational interviews also enabled me to find my way into numerous appealing opportunities to interview with the discriminating companies on my radar, most commonly the immediate employers of my informational interviewing hosts, but also with the employers of their colleagues, in some cases. I fully appreciated the invaluable perspective and guidance that I received in these interviews; I took advantage of the blue-chip resume referrals that came my way as a result.

A particularly enterprising colleague I befriended after I had relocated to New York to commence my post-diploma career utilized the informational interviewing framework almost exclusively during her senior year to round up interviewing privileges with her favored corporate landing spots. She had graduated from a first-class academic program in Washington, DC, that funneled undergraduates by the bushels into Wall Street and other upmarket areas of the East Coast employment landscape. Particularly adept at the art of networking and bestowed with a well-placed alumni network, she scouted the scope of offerings within her campus career services center and went on a handful of interviews on her campus. However, given her specific objectives, she also turned over every rock when it came to networking and fully utilized the treasure trove of names within her pedigreed university alumni network. Ultimately, she wrangled a rich quantity of informational interviews with an army of high-achieving graduates from her school, which ultimately led her to prized formal interviews with many grade-A firms atop her list.

Despite the importance of graduating from a stout undergraduate program and making the grade during your academic career, networking simply remains paramount. Come graduation, it's whom you know—or, perhaps more accurately, whom you may legitimately connect with and recruit to put in a good word on your behalf—that reigns supreme in the steeplechase for topflight employment in today's ultra-competitive labor market.

While I fully investigated the campus interviewing opportunities at my disposal, I secured the vast majority of my interviews—and, ultimately, my first job—via the profound power of networking.

Action Items for Chapter 3:
Conduct an Exhaustive Job Search
Networking

- Exploit your full compass of connections:
    - Respect your contact hierarchy.
    - Tap your second-tier resources.
    - Look for value in your lowest contacts.
- Forge new connections:
    - Cash in on your alumni network.
    - Capitalize on your involvement in group activities.
    - Exploit your geographic origins.
    - Explore social media.
    - Attend on-campus recruiting functions.
    - Attend job fairs and industry events.
    - Pursue informational interviews.

Leveraging Your Internship

Undergraduate internships can represent much more than a wellspring of pre-graduation seasoning and accompanying essential resume filler. Assuming your internship employer offers sufficiently enticing possibilities for career-inaugurating, full-time employment, the firm conceivably yields prime terrain for you to mine for gainful post-commencement opportunities, depending upon your particular circumstances. If the company maintains a need for your entry-level labor and favors an extension of your services as a result of your workplace execution and seamless assimilation into the corporate environment, you potentially need not delve any further in order to nail down a promising future within the professional expanse.

Akin to procuring employment via networking, garnering full-time, post-graduation entry into your internship employer renders advantages for both firm and new hire. From the company perspective, elevating internal candidates into the full-time workforce cuts down on recruiting risk. As I discussed earlier in the chapter, in advancing unseasoned but known commodities into the permanent labor force, employers neutralize the perils and uncertainties inherent in the enlistment of new staff into their full-time domains. The information they maintain on the in-house hopefuls they graduate into their regular ranks ensures that they make the right call in their hiring determinations and greatly diminishes their odds of bringing aboard unsound new recruits. Obviously, employers recruiting outside the firm harbor no such knowledge on the fresh enlistments they reel in and, as a result, assume greater risk. Of course, employers possess no infallible means of predicting the workplace dexterity of applicants drafted externally prior to tendering them binding offers for their services and inking their signatures on the dotted line. Recall from earlier in the chapter the handful of lackluster office mates I rubbed elbows with in the workplace during only two years of service time with my first employer after college. Surely my superiors would have welcomed the opportunity to revisit their original decision making and take a do-over on these regrettable hiring miscues.

Moreover, as I have delineated, rectifying entry-level personnel deficiencies in such fashion enables employers to lock up the services of blue-chip prospects without the customary ensnarement in tiresome, resource-consuming— and by no means flawless—applicant-screening procedures. Promoting qualified in-house candidates from within simply eliminates the need for companies to jump through the usual cumbersome hoops and to commit substantial firm resources to the vetting process for new hires. The streamlined hiring curve that results conserves precious company time and curbs the expenditure of finite financial and human capital.

The kicking upstairs of homegrown hopefuls into the full-time battery also reduces the necessary level of employer investment in their training prior to their deployment to the front company lines. The lion's share of employers, particularly among the more sizeable entities, commonly consign their fresh enlistments into expedient training vehicles prior to their assuming the reins of their new full-time posts. Already more or less acclimated to their workplace environs and up-to-speed on the attendant tasks and responsibilities that come with the territory, the majority of these internal additions to the permanent payroll require only a nominal degree of preparation and refinement. This is particularly true in instances in which the new cadets remain in the same role as before, more or less, within the same company department in which they interned. Others simply progress into full-time positions that resemble a more advanced version of their prior office duties, albeit with a greater scope of responsibilities.

On the other side of the coin, graduating college seniors also reap a bevy of benefits. Primarily, akin to the corporate side of things, undergraduates securing long-term employment though their internship companies also avoid entanglement in the same toilsome interviewing meat grinder. After showing well within the workplace and translating their diligence into firm commitments from their undergraduate employers, these on-the-ball dynamos conveniently sidestep the headache, inconvenience, and stress that invariably accompany the prototypical undergraduate interviewing flight path into the white-collar domain.

Furthermore, after successfully locking down their post-diploma futures in such fashion and bypassing the exhausting corporate filtration mechanism, these ahead-of-the-curve standouts may subsequently relax and ride out the final days of their academic careers comfortably and angst-free, particularly relative to their stress-choked peers still shuffling through their job searches deep into their senior-year campaigns. They arrive at such a position with free time to spare for any remaining academic obligations or other unfinished undergraduate orders of business left on their plates.

Inking tier-one offers of full-time employment via such means also reduces anxiety and bolsters confidence. For undergraduates emerging from their internships with concrete offers but opting to shop their wares to other prospective employers before signing on with their college employers, the situation undoubtedly boosts their self-conviction and, ultimately, their interviewing initiative with the corporate suitors they subsequently engage. In the face of fast-approaching graduation and ensuing christening within the corporate frontier, procuring an operative fallback plan at the outset or amid the early stages of their campaigns certainly stems unease—unease that only crescendos the further they slog without any post-graduation career security. Having an offer in hand builds up their inner assurance, which refines their interviewing performance with other bidders for their services.

After roughly two months of ceaseless canvassing and taxing travel to Manhattan to convene with contacts and prospective suitors, I finally bagged my first frontline offer of employment. Needless to say, prior to gaining entrance into a premium tier of the professional arena, my personal pressure gauge simmered increasingly with each day that passed without having secured a formal contract for my services. Although I never seriously doubted my ability to perform at the next level, seeds of doubt nonetheless threatened to take root on occasion amid my journey, specifically with regard to my ability to realize my lofty employment objectives, and particularly after facing my fair share of rejection and dry patches along the way. Securing entry into the ultracompetitive world of New York City high finance certainly proved to be every bit as challenging as I had originally anticipated, if not more so. However, the instant I received my first offer, I immediately uncorked the champagne and felt a tidal swell of exhilaration and triumph come over me, not to mention a considerably relieved stress level. Furthermore, I positively steamrolled the interviews that I subsequently embarked on. With swelled chest and head up sky-high in the clouds—and also now fully relaxed after having successfully scaled the job-search summit—I unleashed my newly recharged interviewing fire to the fullest and proceeded to ace virtually all of the corporate screenings that I subsequently faced. (Although I ultimately accepted that first offer not long after I had received it, I finished off the remaining interviews on my docket before making the relationship official). My confident, loose disposition simply bred superior all-around interviewing execution, which added to my prospects for additional top-end overtures for my services, had I elected to go that route and seek out other opportunities.

In addition, in sewing up offers of employment from their interning firms, graduating college seniors also pick up a consummate selling point on their candidacies with other potential employers. For individuals graduating from their apprenticeships with concrete tenders for their services in hand yet electing to keep their options open prior to entering into any long-term commitments to these companies, they secure the quintessential feathers in their caps, which they may showcase to any prospective employers they subsequently sit down with. Provided graduates corral these commitments to their services amid the early stages of their campaigns, these ringing third-party endorsements, in addition to rendering enviable fallback plans as they pursue additional, more enticing opportunities elsewhere, unquestionably transmit a strong signal to employers regarding their skill sets and long-term promise. These unambiguous votes of confidence in their abilities from credible third parties cement the merits of their candidacies and alleviate employer concerns, warranted or not, that may otherwise arise regarding their talents. Simply put, the receipt of any such offers early in the process forestalls the raising of any red flags with other corporate suitors encountered down the road.

Although countless undergraduates attain gainful post-graduation employment with entities other than their internship employers without having previously elicited official overtures from their interning firms, exiting your internship without a formal employment invitation conceivably invites greater interviewer scrutiny in the form of some variation of the following obvious question: "If you flashed such potential during your apprenticeship, then why did the higher-ups there allow you to walk out the door without tendering you an official offer to lock up your services long term?" Of course, this excludes any instances in which a pairing of your full-time services with your undergraduate employer remains outside the realm of possibilities for whatever reason—e.g., only short-term in nature, your internship was never intended to last beyond the preset terms of your service, or you simply covet full-time employment within an entirely different sector.

Furthermore, the herd mentality that tends to prevail among corporates works in your favor. Upon their being apprised of your offer (or offers), employers in the mix for your skills routinely follow suit. Fearful of missing the boat on any sought-after talent and eager to jump into the fray, companies, after subjecting you to their own brand of interviewing scrutiny, frequently hop on the bandwagon and offer you a concrete invitation to join their full-time ranks. In other words, as soon as one high-grade employer deems you worthy of passage into its full-time domain and rolls out its welcome mat, your appeal to other suitors picks up steam and, in many instances, spurs them to enter into the bidding and tender you an official invitation to come on board. My mentor always told me that my first real offer of employment would be by far the most challenging to procure, but, once in place, other offers would be sure to follow.

Once I fielded my first big-league employment offer, additional interest in my candidacy quickly snowballed, as if on cue. As a result of the consummate display of faith in my abilities from a top-shelf entity, the tide suddenly shifted in my favor; I quickly became less the outside-looking-in derelict and more the in-demand talent coveted by employers. Sure enough, upon their being made aware of my offer, representatives from other firms grew considerably more receptive to my inquiries and returned correspondence in a much more timely fashion. Most importantly, they grew appreciably more receptive to the idea of bringing me in for interview. Rather than me always being the one pressing for an opportunity—certainly the case prior to my receipt of a competitive bid for my services—hiring managers and human resources personnel then inquired more readily as to when I might be available to sit down with them for an interview. Moreover, upon arrival for cross-examination, I started out my interviews on a higher peg and received greater interviewer favor from the get-go. Ultimately, I entered the corporate interviewing chamber a more credible, interesting prospect, which unquestionably turbo-charged my confidence and my interviewing performance. Rather than remain at the mercy of the company decision makers on the receiving end of my appeals, after the seismic shift, I secured greater control of my post-commencement destiny.

Lastly, undergraduates exiting their apprenticeships with firm commitments to their candidacies in hand gain economic leverage. In rounding up legitimate offers from their undergraduate employers in such fashion, candidates secure timely salary bargaining chips that they may deploy with any subsequent bidders for their post-graduation labor, in certain situations. For example, suppose you elicit an appealing proposal from a first-rate business within your desired field that includes a base pay of $50,000 per year. However, you previously received a more attractive offer from your internship employer to the tune of $55,000 per year, after outpacing expectations and getting along well with virtually everyone in the office. Compensation aside, you ultimately favor the bid from the second courting firm. In such an instance, simply implore suitor number two, in diplomatic fashion, of course, to improve upon its offer, unless such an option clearly remains untenable for whatever reason (e.g., the competing bid comes from a big name industry giant that, as per company protocol, unvaryingly slots each of its of new entry-level workers into exactly the same wage scale without exception). Apprise them of the sweeter deal and petition them, in appropriate tone, of course, to amend the financial terms of their proposition such that they, at a minimum, match up with those of the economically superior offer on the table.

Proceed in such fashion because, in a worst-case scenario, the firm simply rejects your appeal. Assuming you convey your request in a seemly manner and keep it on a professional level, at worst, the company simply declines your proposal but upholds the salary parameters of its original bid.

In order to give yourself the best opportunity to translate your undergraduate internship experience into a fruitful long-term contract from your internship employer, adhere to prevailing firm protocol. Provided you interned under a conventional apprenticeship setup—i.e., a structured affair with an established corporate entity—and the company espouses a receptive philosophy toward the promotion of in-house interns into the full-time domain, convey your interest in remaining with the firm post-graduation to your immediate superiors, human resources staff, or any other appropriate parties prior to the end of your tenure there. If necessary, also supply any required paperwork, and forward the latest and greatest version of your resume to human resources. When utilizing a personal contact or internal liaison to the firm, such as your internship coordinator, simply follow his lead, and comply with whatever measures necessary to enter your name in the mix. For example, if your supervisor directs you to human resources, then follow up with that department. If he refers your resume up the company chain-of-command and routes you to his boss, then obviously follow up with his superior.

Competing for fresh talent, just as undergraduate hopefuls vie for career-inaugurating employment, employers by and large utilize the college-internship vehicle as a means of attracting blue-chip prospects. Capitalizing on relentless undergraduate demand for constructive professional experience, businesses routinely open their corporate doors to astute, career-minded students as a means of promoting their brands and raising their profiles with topflight upperclassmen. Ultimately, crafty businesses aim to entice these sought-after candidates into signing on with their outfits after commencement. From the employer's perspective, intern workplace output during their internships remains largely inconsequential in the grand scheme of things, particularly relative to the gravity of shoring up their entry-level personnel deficits with premium recruits.

Although assertiveness on your part remains critical, you conceivably need exert only scant effort to successfully draw management's attention to your situation. Given the recruiting-oriented nature of collegiate apprenticeships and their more or less root design to supplement the broader corporate recruiting engine with quality prospects, you potentially need only apprise the appropriate parties of your ambition to remain with the firm after graduation to effectively toss your hat in the ring for full-time consideration. In other words, your outstanding job performance on its own can conceivably whet the appetites of hiring powers and render ample motivation for them to offer you full-time employment. Perpetually on alert for promising young hopefuls, employers, as previously noted, invariably take notice when standouts pass through their doors.

You may even earn a concrete, unsolicited offer from your internship employer prior to wrapping up your apprenticeship. Eager to get out in front of the competition and secure the services of any rising stars in their midst, hiring managers may present you with a formal employment invitation prior to your breaking camp with the firm. Your first-rate internship execution alone could conceivably net you a full-time employment offer from your interning firm even without any express intentions on your part. Again, businesses commonly move quickly to lock up the services of ace new kids on the block before any of their competitors enter the picture.

In the event such winds of fortune fail to blow your way or your college employer simply maintains an ambiguous stance regarding the graduation of in-house pupils into its full-time ranks, mine for opportunity anyway. If the top company brass remain noncommittal toward your long-term prospects with the organization, are turtle-slow in divulging their plans, or potentially even come across as chilly to the idea, put out feelers nevertheless. Unless your prospects to gain full-time enlistment with the company after college approximate zero for whatever reason—e.g., you were originally brought in for short-term labor purposes only and the firm maintains no explicit designs for bringing interns into its full-time ranks—rather than automatically assume the company harbors absolutely no room for you on its permanent roster, make every effort nonetheless. Open lines of communication with your internship superior, human resources department, or any other pertinent figures inside the firm who may facilitate your elevation into the long-term workforce.

Relay your interest in signing on for the long haul and push for your inclusion into any company dialogue involving the placement of in-house interns into the permanent company staff because you never know what management may be thinking. Despite a perceived hiring disinclination or lack of transparency on the part of your internship employer regarding its near-term intentions, perhaps the powers-that-be, much to your surprise, value your workplace production and have no qualms at all with the idea of your staying on board in a permanent capacity.

The squeaky wheel gets the grease. Perhaps strategic self-promotion on your part ultimately will tip the scales in your favor and warm the company to the idea of bringing you into the fold full-time.

For example, suppose you intern with a small-scale, reputable boutique during college that maintains only scant surface interest in bringing you or any of your fellow interns back once you earn your diplomas. Despite apathy toward any notion of retaining your services beyond your pre-graduation term of service, after performing well and getting along swimmingly with your co-workers, you nevertheless elect to take your best shot and punctuate your expectation-eclipsing production and sturdy rapport with your office mates with an ambitious campaign to sell the company generals on your long-term potential with the firm and, ultimately, the idea of extending your internship into a full-fledged role. Perhaps the combination of your office dexterity and deft intra-firm maneuvering swings the pendulum your way and impels management to make room for you on its permanent roster after graduation.

Without any outspokenness on your part, such an opportunity most likely never materializes. Given the firm's indifference towards the idea of promoting from within and hiring homegrown interns, your post-diploma narrative plays out differently in the absence of your politicking. In all likelihood, you simply part ways with your internship employer upon the completion of your internship obligations, effectively passing up a gainful, full-time opportunity in the process. Capping your internship output with well-timed, diplomatic campaigning potentially forestalls a divergence of your post-apprenticeship path from that of your internship employer and conceivably represents the difference between your rustling up a primo, career-flowering opportunity or not.

Telegraphing your ambition only aids your cause. Some undergraduates may fear coming across as a bother to employers and, as a result, dial back their aggressiveness. While it may run counter to common undergraduate practice, in actuality, signaling your initiative and spreading around your desire to ink a long-term deal with your internship employer actually elevates your stock in the eyes of management. If the ball ultimately rolls your way and long-term employment with the firm becomes a realistic option, displaying hunger and assertively lobbying your bosses ultimately vaults you up the company's shopping list and places you in the best position to seize any long-term opportunities. Unquestionably, employers value drive and initiative within new recruits.

In the event your internship employer remains receptive to the idea of your continuing on with the company post-commencement, but on the surface has no room for you on its permanent roster, simply nudge the appropriate company parties to consider you for full-time employment regardless. If your college employer appreciates your contributions and deems you an asset to the firm worthy of a spot on its full-time squad, but unfortunately has no evident entry-level openings for you to lay claim to once you finish your degree (e.g., the firm is a niche industry player that simply lacks the scale to regularly dip into the undergraduate labor pool and hires fresh enlistments only intermittently), refrain from throwing in the towel just yet and canvass for your appropriation onto the regular payroll. Rather than remain on the sideline and fail to follow up on any intra-firm opportunities at all, broach the topic of your remaining with the firm to the appropriate parties, even in the face of the seemingly long odds.

However, rather than petition for a specific entry-level post in this case, simply campaign from a different angle. Given the lack of apparent entry-level opportunities in such a scenario, announce your desire to remain with the firm, but adopt an outside-the-box approach and push for your annexation into the full-time staff via inventive means. For example, propose that the firm simply spin your current role into a permanent position replete with full-time responsibilities and corresponding full-time wages, or, alternatively, press your higher-ups to chisel a newfangled, full-scale post for you. Given your favorable standing with co-workers and management, perhaps your superiors may mint a newfound frontline role for you after all. If the firm truly values your abilities and recognizes your long-term potential, the powers-that-be may very well find a way to slot you into their long-range plans, present hiring needs aside. Recall my earlier commentary on widespread employer inclination to pounce on any standout candidates that enter the picture. Simply pitch any clever ideas that may coerce your company higher-ups into keeping you on board after graduation.

In the event an earlier internship has already wrapped and a meaningful amount of time has passed since you last spoke with anyone at the company, remain on the offensive and resuscitate correspondence. Reach out, and restart dialogue with your former internship coordinator or any other relevant figures from your tenure that may conceivably assist you in exploring long-term possibilities with the firm. Look into any possibility, however slim, of your catching on in a full-time role.

Do not allow an opportunity to pass you by because neither you nor your undergraduate employer ever made an attempt to explore the possibility of your becoming a full-time member of the crew. Even if permanent employment with the company appears to be a long shot, entertain all possible options. Echoing a prior motif, you certainly have nothing to lose by asking.

Only the most vocal, visibly ambitious interns stand the best chance to gain long-range opportunities with their undergraduate employers. The ahead-of-the-game dynamos who not only shine within the workplace but also convey a keen interest in locking down long-term employment remain the best bets to convince the company brass to reward their pre-graduation service time with a firm invitation to sign on post-diploma.

One of my best friends from college successfully translated his college internship into a productive, career-budding role with his undergraduate employer in the face of a murky hiring picture. After achieving within the workplace as an undergraduate, in addition to meshing well with his office mates and forging robust workplace relationships along the way, he diplomatically leaned on his superiors to reward his efforts with a long-term employment invitation. He harbored no knowledge of the company's undergraduate recruiting designs for the current school year, yet, favoring a continuation of his tenure there, he petitioned undaunted. Despite no real read on his long-range career prospects with the firm, he campaigned aggressively until finally hitting pay dirt and eliciting concrete reciprocation of his interest in the form of an official full-time offer. More than pleased with the outcome, he accepted the offer in short order, turning down a competitive offer he had previously received from a prominent consulting firm. Although virtually all of my university peers and fellow first-years from my first job in the professional domain have since moved on from their internships and their first post-college jobs (certainly a notable outcome considering the small army of fresh undergraduates enlisted by my employer during that calendar year), to this day, my university comrade remains gainfully employed by the same company that he apprenticed under during college

No one else is going to petition management on your behalf. Although you may very well elicit a measure of endorsement or assistance from other company employees in some form or fashion during your journey, neither your internship coordinator nor any other wage earners within the company are going to take it upon themselves to press the company brass for you, particularly in the absence of any aggressiveness on your part. Operate under the assumption that you can rely on no one else to seize the reins and move your initiative forward. As with anything, you alone shoulder the burden of opening your own doors to opportunity.

Action Items for Chapter 3:
Conduct an Exhaustive Job Search
Leveraging Your Internship

- Adhere to prevailing firm protocol.
- Convey your interest to the firm.
- Mine for opportunities irrespective of the circumstances.
- Open lines of communication with your internship superior, HR department, or other pertinent figures.

Cold Calling

Cold calling means reaching out to employers unsolicited in order to inquire about full-time employment opportunities. You maintain no meaningful ties or prior relationships with any of the entities you canvass. You have enlisted no connections or other third parties to intervene on your behalf. You have no knowledge of the hiring aims of the firms you approach, or such information simply remains irrelevant, as you intend to pursue dialogue with them, in any event. Rather than restricting your opportunities to only those explicitly on the table—e.g., only interviewing with the businesses recruiting at your school or responding to appealing employment listings posted online—leave nothing undone, and petition as many upper-tier companies as possible. Irrespective of whether or not they are hiring, circulate your candidacy to as extensive an upmarket corporate audience as possible, and widen your prospects to secure coveted interviewing privileges with esteemed employers.

Although not necessarily a first-line means of scouting for post-college opportunity, particularly relative to other, more expedient plans of attack, such as campus interviewing and networking, cold calling first-class employers represents a viable route to register your candidacy on the recruiting radars of quality proprietors, for several reasons. Primarily, cold calling conceivably represents your only path to certain employers. Contacting grade-A entities outside of your university, prior affiliation, or timely third-party facilitation potentially represents your only chance at introducing your resume to the top-end employers on your post-graduation shopping list, given the inherent limitations of other, more opportune job-search strategies. For example, campus interviewing only introduces you to a finite universe of suitors, and, furthermore, your well of personal contacts is sure to run dry or yield diminishing marginal returns at some point as your second- and third-tier contacts offer less and less value. Only so many companies may recruit at your school during the senior-year recruiting season, and your individual contacts may connect you with only so many expedient resources.

As I touched on earlier in this chapter, upper-ranking firms by and large farm only select university fields for fresh blue-chip talent. Given their first-tier standing among the broader corporate hierarchy, incessant inundation with competitive undergraduate resumes, desire to remain atop the professional totem, and simple logistics, the distinguished firms on your radar may not necessarily recruit at your school. These enterprises generally have the ability to pick and choose when it comes to undergraduate recruiting and need not necessarily promote themselves on campus in order to attract premium university talent. In the absence of any personal tie-ins or other means of drawing their attention, you conceivably have no other way to stir up dialogue and ultimately obtain employment with companies on your wish list of preferred employers.

Second, cold calling entails no restrictions. Operating within such a boundless plan of attack affords you the latitude to play the numbers game full-on and to sweep through sought-after firms at your own ambitious, unrelenting pace—provided you make your pitch during normal working hours, you may cold call virtually any company at any time. Canvassing on your own outside of conventional job-search guardrails allows you to disseminate your resume to a near-countless quantity of A-1 employers across numerous industries and geographic locales over the course of your campaign. As I have already highlighted, of course, the more businesses you approach and the more resumes you circulate, the greater your chances of drawing corporate attention to your candidacy.

Simply put, cold calling allows you to be as proactive as you want to be. You need not wait around for any specific dates or preset campus interviewing times to pop up on the calendar before initiating contact. You need not passively wait for the proverbial green light from a personal contact or resume referrer as they work their magic with their employers before you float your initial feelers. You dictate which companies you wish to pursue. To a certain extent, you dictate your opportunities.

Lastly, canvassing on your own alleviates your dependence upon traditional employment search channels. Rather than remain at the mercy of the caliber of offerings within your other, higher-priority plans of attack, cold calling diminishes the gravity of these avenues to your campaign. In the event the opportunities up for grabs within the more straightforward job-search strategies remain limited, leave much to be desired in terms of quality, or simply come up short relative to your ambitions, contacting premium entities out of the blue in such fashion enables you to potentially overcome such impediments.

In order to get cracking and cold call with the best of them, grab your phone and call the full list of corporate targets on your radar. Employing the Internet as a primary wellhead of information, put together a master list of the companies that you wish to work for, including a deep inventory of first-tier choices and second-tier alternatives, in descending order of importance—it's best to formulate an operative fallback plan because your top choices are certainly no shoo-ins to turn out in your favor. Telephone with abandon, and fire off your resume to as many desirable businesses as possible, irrespective of their undergraduate recruiting designs. All upmarket employers on your radar should receive a copy of your resume, particularly the more sizeable entities that employ large numbers of employees at any given time and therefore must dip into the university labor pool with routine frequency. Cast aside any pre-call anxieties you may have, implement an unremitting, no-holds-barred modus operandi, and start smiling and dialing.

Amid my own job-search odyssey during my final year of college, I cold called countless employers and dispensed my resume by the truckload. Intent on bombarding the professional sphere with copies of my resume and broadcasting my candidacy to as many top-end firms as possible, and in addition to networking extensively and embarking upon campus interviews in quantity, I picked up the receiver and rang untold numbers of upper-ranking firms and up-to-par, second-choice outfits on a near-daily basis. Although I encountered a heavy dose of rejection, at least from the companies that bothered to give me the time of day and acknowledge my inquiries in the first place, I kept my nose to the grindstone and fought through the seemingly endless corporate dismissals of my efforts. I plugged away until I finally rounded up coveted interviews with a number of the respectable firms that I had targeted for post-commencement enlistment. I set the bar high, channeling the vast majority of my exertions toward the greener employment pastures of New York City. However, although I wielded a competitive candidacy, I simply did not anticipate the acute, unrelenting helping of the ice-cold corporate shoulder and utter apathy to my application that I came up against.

To this day, I maintain a collection of rejection letters from a number of the acclaimed entities that I pursued. Ornamented in majestic fashion with decorous, type-written corporate letterhead, each and every one of these ceremonious brush-off notices graciously thanked me for my interest in their business but then delivered their final judgments in terse, polished, yet somewhat amusing fashion—amusing only in hindsight, that is—along the lines of the following: "… however, we regret to inform you that we simply do not have any available full-time opportunities befitting of your skill set at this time." As if fit alone represented the only obstacle to my recruitment into their esteemed enterprises, rather than their apparently less-than-perfect impressions of my candidacy relative to the fierce competition I squared off against. The puffed-up company-speak was invariably followed by the customary hollow corporate sendoff: "… however, we wish you the best of luck in your future endeavors."

Despite these tribulations, it all worked out in the end for me. Although I secured the bulk of my interviews via other strategies, I nonetheless achieved my objective of reeling in a serviceable quantity of interviewing opportunities with blue-ribbon employers via unsolicited cold calling, unquestionably an improvement to my ultimate prospects for success.

Perhaps no scenario, however, illustrates the merits of cold calling more so than the case of a young intern I crossed paths with during my first full-time professional position after graduation.

One day, during a random, hectic work week, an energetic young figure decked in a dapper suit and tie suddenly materialized at my desk in order to introduce himself and volunteer his services should I require assistance with any of the tasks on my plate. After reciprocating his courtesies and introducing myself, I engaged him briefly in cordial conversation and gained deeper insight behind the bearer of this eager, naive face before me. Currently enrolled in his final year of college at a notable nearby academic institution, he simply wished to acquaint himself with his new office mates and make the rounds during his first day on the job. Slated to graduate in one more year, he explained that he had successfully secured an internship stint with the firm, set to run for a predetermined period of approximately three months, mirroring our undergraduate summer internship program. Perplexed by this seemingly random addition to the company payroll given that our standard undergraduate internship program had already wrapped a couple of months prior at summer's end, I asked about his rather unorthodox trajectory into the company payroll. Specifically, I inquired as to how he had managed to pull off such an impressive stunt and engineer his own one-man, pre-graduation term of service with the firm, no doubt a sought-after experience for ambitious college students. Our regular summer student internship program presented a formidable if not impossible task to begin with during the regular sign-up period, let alone earning passage entirely outside of conventional company practice. He responded by informing me that he simply pounded the pavement and canvassed virtually every corner of the white-collar expanse, irrespective of firm-hiring status or procedure, until finally knocking the socks off my employer and arriving at our present destination.

Despite the fact that my firm had for all intents and purposes already shuttered its doors to undergraduate interns for the current recruiting season, this fearless college upstart somehow managed to charm his way into our esteemed offices, successfully circumventing conventional apprentice-hiring protocol in the process, an exceedingly challenging proposition, to be sure. Utterly unfazed by his grim prospects at the outset to carry out such a tour de force and gain admittance into the firm on any level, and absolutely hell-bent on snaring a prime resume-building opportunity with a noteworthy outfit prior to graduation, he scratched and clawed until finally catching his big break and striking apprenticeship gold. With commendable resume in hand and compelling sales pitch on the tip of his tongue, this dynamic young fireball, despite his complete lack of seasoning or prior dealings with the professional sphere, stopped at nothing. He hammered away at the ocean of potential corporate landing spots until he finally nailed down a prime pre-graduation role with my employer.

Although this may not exactly reflect your particular set of circumstances, the same lesson applies. Take a swing, or several swings for that matter, and cold call each and every premium firm in your post-graduation sights.

Cold calling certainly has a place on your senior-year agenda. Despite its second-tier distinction and accompanying inferior hit rate, at least with sought-after employers, reaching out without any prior personal or campus ties to the entities you petition remains a viable approach in your search for your future. Although not necessarily a surefire strategy, and by no means a walk in the park given the typical corporate response and accompanying kicks in the teeth that invariably come with the territory, cold calling remains an investigable means of scouting for A-1, post-college opportunities, particularly after exhausting your principal courses of action.

Action Items for Chapter 3:
Conduct an Exhaustive Job Search
Cold Calling

- Assemble a master list of A-1 firms.
- Telephone with abandon and submit your resume to as many top-end firms as possible.

Utilizing Recruiters

Recruiting firms serve as intermediaries between professionals and the corporate sphere. Ranging in scale from lean and specialized to elephantine and all-encompassing, these enterprises unearth, prescreen—typically via their own firsthand appraisal—and ultimately pair qualified candidates with apt employers. For example, on one end of the spectrum, high-end executive search firms place only senior professionals at the top of the white-collar food chain. On the other end of the spectrum, sizeable, diverse outfits route workers of all seasoning levels into all manner of corporate landing spots. Although historically a more relevant resource for individuals with some measure of professional experience under their belts, these conduits to the corporate sphere are yet another viable avenue to connect your candidacy with frontline businesses.

Enlisting staffing firms to go to work for you affords you a wash of advantages. First off, these entities maintain primo access to the white-collar arena. They know which firms are hiring and in which sectors. After appraising your resume and sizing you up in person, they may refer you directly to gainful opportunity with top-shelf employers in your targeted sector.

Second, the abundance of players in the space undoubtedly works in your favor. The excess of enterprises in the business of marrying employers and employees allows you to contact a near-countless quantity of outfits in the corporate matchmaking trade. Although the majority may not necessarily cater to rookie wage earners in pursuit of their first big-league gigs, given their visibility and accessibility to the professional workforce, you may conceivably align yourself with a serviceable quantity that may agree to take up your plight and promote your candidacy to premium employers. A plentiful sum of these third-party facilitators for your campaign remain only a telephone call away.

Third, due to the nature of their trade, these specialists naturally pick up a vested interest in your future. These brokers to the corporate world earn their livelihood upon the successful placement of competent candidates into suitable corporate destinations. They receive compensation from their white-collar clientele—you incur no cash outlay in mobilizing them to maneuver on your behalf—so if you are a great fit, they have every incentive to pitch your skill set to corporates as aggressively as possible. The tying of their personal economics to your success renders more than ample stimulus for them to go to bat for you and to ultimately marry you off to a top-notch business.

Lastly, headhunters might very well impart timely employment-specific insight that furthers your operation. As a result of their regular engagement with and proximity to hiring firms, they maintain a firm read on the pulse of the labor market at any given time. Namely, they have a bead on which sectors and which employers in particular may house hiring needs at the entry level, and they may therefore know of fitting opportunities for you to pursue. Consequently, even in the event the companies they have in mind for you bear no current employment openings for graduating college seniors, or they only facilitate the placement of seasoned professionals, these outfits may nonetheless enlighten you on up-to-date, employer-specific intelligence that leads you to blue-chip opportunity elsewhere. They may key you in on sectors and potential employers beyond their immediate scope that have openings appropriate for your experience. For example, although she cannot route you directly to any hiring firms in her wheelhouse, a recruiter points you to a handful of under-the-radar startups and other early-stage businesses in need of fresh entry-level talent. At a minimum, perhaps these third-party intermediaries may offer to hold a copy of your resume on file and notify you in the event any relevant employment opportunities come across their desks.

In order to sally forth and recruit a gang of recruiting firms to take up your cause, sweep through the full range of participants in the field. Just as with cold calling, employ the World Wide Web as a primary information wellhead. With input from your mentor, peers, and acquaintances, come up with a wall-to-wall list of all the relevant inhabitants of the space. Echoing a familiar theme, invoke a sweeping plan of attack and play the numbers game full force—contact each and every one of these potential agents for your campaign.

Upon connection, relay your situation. Inform them of your impending graduation and corresponding quest for entry into the professional expanse, and inquire as to whether or not they can be of assistance. In the event they cannot match you with any top-end firms themselves, simply ask if they may possibly route you in the direction of any other dynamic opportunities or if they harbor any knowledge at all of any other relevant ground-level opportunities on par with your objectives. Let them know that intel on any specific segments of the business arena that are possibly conducive to graduating college seniors would be particularly appreciated. Even though only a minority of these recruiters might deal in the placement of undergraduates, reach out, in any event. Perhaps a receptive headhunter or two may receive your overtures favorably and let you in on timely corporate hiring information that ultimately steers you in the direction of appealing employment opportunity elsewhere.

After delivering your sales pitch and snaring a receptive ear, put your best foot forward in any subsequent dealings with recruiters. If you make the cut past the initial phone call and score meetings in their offices, approach the situation just as you would with a priority employer. Much like a job interview, an office meeting provides for a more intensive appraisal of your candidacy, which will need to be satisfactory before they refer you to any of their corporate clientele. After assuming ownership of the initial screening process, the recruiter often then takes a back seat, acquainting you with the appropriate employer directly and leaving you to interview with that firm, akin to any other corporate courtships you may enter into. Dress to impress, tote extra copies of your resume, and, most importantly, convey your initiative, self-assuredness, and preparedness to enter the professional sphere. Present yourself in a seemly, upright manner, and sell these potential facilitators on your aptitude. Demonstrate your ambition, and convince them of your viability as a candidate so they have no qualms whatsoever about endorsing your skill set to frontline employers. In certain instances, you may bypass this step altogether and meet with the underlying employers directly, without having first met with the headhunters. For example, if he is already comfortable with your resume and your overall presentation after having digested your resume and scrutinized your candidacy over the telephone, a recruiter may simply cut to the chase and introduce you to the particular corporate clientele they have in mind for you, even without having screened you in person beforehand.

I connected with my second employer after college via the recruiting firm medium. The cessation of my two-year term of service was looming on the horizon, and I required formal invitation to remain with the firm beyond two years because a continuation of my tenure was not fully guaranteed. Second-year financial analysts in my position either applied for a third year, ventured off to graduate school in pursuit of their Master of Business Administration degrees, or sought out other gigs elsewhere. So, I explored my options outside the firm and eventually stumbled upon a prime opportunity. This came via an employer-promulgated employment listing from a select website, and it brought me face-to-face with a top-drawer headhunter.

After responding to the posting online, I received a fact-finding telephone call from a recruiter. Brought on board to spearhead the recruiting effort—that is, sorting through prospects and overseeing the initial interviewing process—on behalf of a niche-asset-management outfit, this first-class intermediary summoned me to its center of operations to audition for the position. After showcasing my wares to the team of staffing firm interviewers assigned to my case and surviving their cordial but thorough line of questioning, I advanced to a formal interview with the underlying employer. Behind the scenes up until now, this employer had authored the initial employment listing and had retained the headhunting firm to connect them with a junior-level recruit with at least two years of first-rate seasoning in the financial services arena for a financial analyst position within their modest operation. Incentivized to consummate the transaction and collect payment for their services, but also mindful of the need to expedite an apt pairing, the recruiting firm and its staff proved to be a very professional and accommodating liaison over the course of the affair. Managing the courtship with precision, streamlining the process, and saving both me and my eventual employer a ton of time and hassle, this expedient matchmaker functioned as a well-oiled machine.

Working professionals routinely field unprompted telephone calls from aggressive headhunters, as these competitive outfits constantly plot to drum up new business and unearth grade-A prospects for their clients. This is certainly standard recruiting firm practice, particularly in fast-paced corners of the business arena such as New York City. Indeed, my working peers and I were regularly in contact with them on some level after college, and I engaged numerous recruiters throughout my career. Particularly after graduating from school and breaking into the fast-moving world of high finance in Manhattan, an obvious hotbed of white-collar employer-to-employer migration and a bustling hub for professional headhunters to operate, I gained a deeper appreciation for the headhunting intermediary and its contributions to the corporate hiring wheel.

Although headhunters reach out to veteran operatives in the professional workforce in the most common scenario—either to feel them out or to facilitate referrals on behalf of corporate clients—you may certainly seize the reins and contact them yourself to inquire about opportunities. Seeking to climb the corporate ladder or simply in need of a change of scenery, workers at all levels of the white-collar spectrum take advantage of the headhunting channel as a means of getting their names out there and connecting with top-tier employers.

Action Items for Chapter 3:
Conduct an Exhaustive Job Search
Utilizing Recruiters

- Sweep through the full range of participants in the space.
- Explain your situation.
- Put your best foot forward.

Scouring Employment Listings

Scouring employment listings pertains to combing through job postings outside of those already catalogued within your campus career services center. Disseminated by employers in the market for fresh undergraduate recruits—or, in some cases, by recruiting firms on behalf of corporate clients—these notices highlight the core essentials of the positions entailed and not much else. Preferring to dictate the terms of any ensuing correspondence with interested applicants, the businesses behind these ads, particularly those taking up residence within the upper rim of the professional arena, frame a quick snapshot of the outstanding particulars of the full-time spots up for grabs. They typically offer up a company e-mail address and scant other details. In many cases, they even explicitly instruct applicants to use the designated e-mail address for resume submission purposes only—i.e., no telephone calls, e-mails with questions, or any other inquiries into the firm at all. Such practice affords employers the autonomy to manage their own recruiting ships. In addition to confining the ensuing dialogue to only those prospects whose resumes pass inspection and whose candidacies ultimately warrant further scrutiny in the form of first-round interviews, laying down specific ground rules in such fashion also prevents employers from wasting precious time with subpar candidates. Moreover, implementing such an approach forestalls any overly zealous characters from taking advantage of the situation and hounding company staff with inordinate besiegement, such as incessantly bombarding the company with annoying telephone calls in order to inquire about entry-level opportunities. Although a lower priority strategy in your job-search toolkit, thumbing through employment listings renders another viable means of scouring the corporate expanse for gainful, career-inaugurating opportunities.

In order to shake the most fruit out of this tree, traverse the relevant resources at your disposal in comprehensive fashion. Scour the Internet, but also appeal to your mentor, peers, acquaintances, and anyone else who may point you in the direction of any favorable websites to navigate (or any favorable print media, for that matter). Narrow your hunting grounds to only those corners of the Internet with postings pertinent to graduating college seniors in search of their first full-time gigs. After rooting out the best sites, echoing a familiar theme, invoke a sweeping plan of attack, and fire off your resume to any and all first-rate opportunities that catch your eye.

Be selective with the sites you frequent, however. Exercise discretion, and skip over any generic or unfiltered information superhighway territory more or less open to all and bloated with substandard opportunities unbefitting of a productive college graduate. Waste no time or energy sorting through the whirl of run-of-the-mill listings that offer no or only marginal upside, such as generic online classified ads from your local newspaper. Stick to the stretches of cyberspace geared toward your particular objectives, or at least to those areas comprising a decent amount of applicable entry-level opportunities for goal-oriented graduating college seniors. Distinguished businesses rarely employ middling or unrefined media to conduct their recruiting business.

Comply with any and all instructions outlined in the solicitations you pursue. If an employer explicitly requests that all applicants apply online or remit their resumes via e-mail only, then, of course, respect such wishes and submit your one-pager in electronic format where and how requested. Refrain from transmitting your resume or reaching out in any other fashion. Although aggressiveness and persistence typically yield the biggest rewards in the job-search game, disregarding proper protocol—e.g., in an ill-conceived strategy to highlight your enterprise and draw attention to your candidacy—invariably repels employers and diminishes your chances of success. For example, hounding your prospect with an excessive number of phone calls or other ill-conceived strategies draws negative attention to your candidacy. Ignoring established decorum raises red flags with employers and spurs company decision makers to strike your application from consideration entirely.

Persistence is one thing, but flouting simple rules of conduct is another. Tread on the right side of the fine line between enterprising and overaggressive. Use good form, and fall in line with the preferred procedure. When it comes to registering your interest with employers, take no unnecessary risks.

When dealing with top-shelf companies, it's more than common for several days to pass after submitting an application without hearing anything back at all. If this happens, follow up with a telephone call or e-mail. Without crossing any lines and harassing employers with pesky e-mails or telephone implorations, reach out again to the companies you initially offered your resume. Make sure you are not in violation of any specific company requests with respect to their application instructions, and restrict yourself to only one or maybe two follow-up inquiries—even two may be pushing it. If your overtures still go unreturned, rather than continue to bark up the same tree, simply move on to the ocean of other worthwhile opportunities that await your pursuit.

I sorted through countless employment notices over the course of my senior-year quest. After getting the ball rolling within my top job-search plans of attack—namely, networking and campus interviewing—I directed ample attention to the scores of listings in cyberspace. After focusing my energy on the relevant resources and foraging through—and periodically re-foraging through—these areas in search of fresh opportunities, I filed my resume with as many frontline businesses as possible. Although a less-expedient means of connecting with upmarket employers relative to my best job-search strategies, I beat the bushes until finally connecting with a serviceable quantity of first-tier suitors for my services. Despite the drudgery, the tortoise-like pace at times, and sparse hit rate, at least with the top-shelf businesses on my radar, I ultimately achieved my end-game objective of upgrading my odds of emerging from my efforts with a prized offer of full-time employment in hand.

Action Items for Chapter 3:
Conduct an Exhaustive Job Search
Scouring Employment Listings

- Explore each of the relevant resources at your disposal.
- Be selective with the websites you frequent.
- Comply with all outlined instructions.

Working for Free

In certain instances, you might consider working for free. After exhausting your full sweep of job-search plans of attack, as a last and decidedly final resort, you may elect to contract your post-college services to a first-tier employer without compensation. In such a scenario, you sign up for an unpaid, short-term or possibly open-ended role with a topflight firm—enlisting with anything less defeats the purpose—in a last-ditch effort to make an impression and get your foot in the door. Given the shortage of other options at this juncture, rather than simply pack it in and settle for a lesser opportunity beneath your personal bar, you forego near-term pay in order to salvage your situation and at least stay in the game. This is akin to taking on an unsalaried internship with a respectable firm prior to graduation in a bid to fatten your resume and gain much-needed experience. Provided all goes well and your gamble pays off, you translate this trial into a profitable long-term post within the same firm. In this case, your exemplary performance spurs management to elevate you into a permanent, fully compensated position. Alternatively, you might leverage the resume-building stint into a sought-after position elsewhere. Although not an attractive option for every graduating college senior struggling to locate gainful post-college employment, such a bold strategy represents a viable alternative if all else fails in your bid to land primo employment.

Even though working for free is clearly short of your original vision for your immediate post-graduation career, such a move potentially represents your best course of action for a host of rationales. Primarily, in swallowing your pride and venturing down such an ambitious path, you keep your long-term candidacy intact. Rather than blight your track record by remaining on the shelf for an extended period after college and creating a conspicuous, candidacy-debasing gap on your resume or, perhaps worse, by softening your standards and entering into any measure of employment shy of your preferred grade, forfeiting your short-term economics in favor of the bigger picture preserves the integrity of your credentials and your marketability to future suitors for your services. Canvassing for topflight, permanent employment while under the umbrella of an A-1 employer, even in a transient, salary-bereft capacity, unquestionably trumps graduating and searching for top-end employment while rounding out the unemployment line or while taking up residence within a lower-tier outfit.

Overemphasizing the present and prioritizing your short-term finances over the long-term health of your candidacy comes at a price. Embracing any measure of subpar employment in a departure from your original senior-year blueprint unquestionably puts your long-term prospects at risk with upper-ranking firms. For example, suppose in the wake of an ineffective job search, despite success in school and a praiseworthy resume, you throw in the towel and pick up a part-time bartending job at a local restaurant in a short-sighted move to rectify your unanticipated unemployment and to shore up your immediate cash flow situation. While seemingly innocuous on the surface, such a near-sighted measure stains your appeal with top-end employers and jeopardizes your long-term candidacy. Such a questionable decision simply sends the wrong message to frontline businesses. Why would a diligent student feel the need to make such a move? A truly competent hopeful would not allow himself to veer off course in such fashion. Topflight employers remain averse to bringing aboard anyone who would sell themselves short in such a way.

Second, the radical step of working for free buys you much-needed time. At the end of your rope after striking out in your push to sign on with a first-string employer after graduation, augmenting your qualifications with a stint of constructive service time with a primo operation, even if impermanent in nature and devoid of regular wages, keeps your ship afloat with upper-tier firms until you figure out your next move. (Of course, you need not mark such an experience as "unpaid" on your resume; the name of a solid employer on your resume is what other employers notice, after all.) Any evident stretch of inactivity or unproductivity on your post-graduation ledger undoubtedly befouls your candidacy in the minds of first-class employers. Furthermore, the greater the void, the more harmful it is to your campaign. Pursuing full-time employment with top-end employers immediately after graduation with a fully intact resume poses no issues with hiring managers relative to the prospect of ringing up discriminating employers for opportunities six months out. Blue-chip candidates bear no such discernible holes in their timelines.

Lastly, the greater proximity to the professional sphere fosters circumstances conducive for networking. Filling in your time sheet within an upmarket, white-collar environment—a superb breeding ground for forging primo fresh connections—day in, day out, even without pay, places you in prime position to mint newfangled relationships with forefront professionals. You could develop a rapport with both junior and veteran wage earners alike, either of which may make for timely allies for your campaign. Given the circumstances, cultivating new connections may prove invaluable, particularly in the event you fail to catch on with the company long term and require a helping hand to break into another premium employer.

In order to corral such a capacity, scour the landscape in wall-to-wall fashion. Similar to any other job-search strategy you pursue, throw numbers at the equation, and petition company after company and contact after contact. Pick up where you left off from your regular senior-year operation, and retrace your prior steps, first and foremost. Beginning with your primary undergraduate internship, or internships, circle back with the relevant figures from the company(s) you apprenticed under during college. That is, reach out to individuals such as your internship coordinator or other weighty corporate personnel that you became acquainted with over the course of your tenure with the company. Rather than fruitlessly revive worn-out dialogue centering on a potential long-term future for you with your employers, break the ice on the subject of your returning to the firm in an uncompensated, internship-type role.

Next, call on each of your personal contacts once more. Revisit your full book of familiar connections plus any recent additions to your contact file that you got to know during your first sweep through the professional sphere. For example, look to frontline employees, human resources staff, or any other relevant company personnel or crucial individuals that brokered your introduction to their employers, and float the idea of them bringing you into the fold in the aforementioned unconventional capacity.

Update each of these individuals on your situation, and convey your willingness to embrace such a position. Brief them on your current state of affairs, including any near misses with noteworthy companies or, conversely, any offers of note that you walked away from. Apprise them of your revised objectives, and reference your prior swim through their company doors, where applicable—i.e., instances in which you have already interviewed with their employers for regular full-time employment consideration. Inform them of your current plan to bite the bullet and find a home with a premium employer in a reduced role, even if it means taking on a temporary, uncompensated duty. Air your suitability for such an ambitious proposition, and float the idea of your signing on with their businesses only for the experience.

After re-exploring familiar terrain, cast your net wider in your pursuits. In light of your shortage of other options at this point, and the fact that you only require some measure of first-order resume filler with a reputable company in order to prolong your window with upper-crust employers, expand your scope to encompass a more expansive orbit of short-term destinations. Reopen lines of communication with the appropriate parties from the first-string employers atop your original post-graduation wish list, but also check in with the volumes of first-rate businesses outside of your original compass of favored landing spots. Call on the mountain of companies across the white-collar spectrum that, although not necessarily in line with your first-choice preferences, nonetheless offer a more than sufficient alternative at this juncture. You need not necessarily conjure up permanent opportunity with your dream employer at this time. Rather than confining yourself to only hard-to-get, high-grade opportunities, extending your shelf life simply trumps all at this late stage in the ballgame.

As I previously noted, relay your resolve to any and all of the people you approach. Irrespective of the individual you solicit, or re-solicit in some cases, whether he or she is a familiar face or a figure with whom you maintain only scant or no prior familiarity, telegraph your fervor and your bound determination to earn passage into the top of the professional food chain. Perhaps your gumption wins you favor. Perhaps, even though you missed the cut the first time around, your grit and perseverance—and maybe a timely assist from a personal contact—tip the scales in your favor and drive one of these businesses to recognize your potential and carve out a spot for you.

Upper-tier employers have no incentive to bring aboard unassertive prospects in a conventional full-time role, much less for any type of unorthodox capacity outside of the normal practice, even in situations devoid of compensation. If employers are to deviate from regular hiring norms and make an exception, then it would surely be only for the young fireballs that not only impress on paper but also display robust inner drive in the face of job-search tribulation—in other words, the visibly ambitious, qualified pupils who, for whatever reason, simply came up short during their regular job searches. Bringing your "A game" and convincing corporates of your wherewithal and superior skill set remain your only chance at landing such an opportunity.

Recall the example from earlier in the chapter in which a tireless young intern successfully edged his way into my employer via an entirely unconventional path. Despite the gale-force headwinds—namely, the prior cessation of our regular undergraduate internship program for the current year, surely his best shot to break into the company otherwise—this impressive up-and-comer remained undaunted. He was unfazed by his low, or in this case, nonexistent standing in the professional hierarchy, yet he somehow overcame the odds and found his way into a fruitful stint with my employer.

Although I achieved my ultimate objective and secured a prized offer from a preferred employer before commencement, and therefore didn't need to venture down such a path, I certainly would have considered taking such extreme action had I deemed it necessary to keep my original game plan alive and kicking. I had an ardent commitment to my long-term employment designs, an unwillingness to back off my standards, and an unflagging conviction in my aptitude and in my ability to thrive in the corporate arena. So, even when confronted with a discouraging job search in which I certainly struck out on my fair share of occasions and that dragged on longer than I had originally anticipated, I absolutely would have entertained the idea of contracting out my post-graduation labor to a distinguished business over the alternative of resigning myself to a subpar fate with a ho-hum employer. I would have done this in the short run even at the expense of a much anticipated major league paycheck.

Even though far from a sure thing and hardly an ideal means of cutting your teeth in the professional domain, take the plunge, and pursue such a drastic move if the situation warrants. Provided you boast the necessary skill and resolve to see such a solution through, and provided, of course, you remain undaunted in your bid for a full-time, paying gig, even in the face of crushing job-search storm and stress, abstain from loosening your standards, and pursue passage into the top end of the corporate landscape by whatever means necessary. Place no shackles on your potential to realize your near- and long-term career objectives, despite a possible lack of positive developments on the job-search front. Stay the course, forge ahead, and think outside the box. Challenging times simply call for strategic, forward-thinking measures.

Action Items for Chapter 3:
Conduct an Exhaustive Job Search
Working for Free

- Scour the full landscape of relevant, top-shelf firms.
- Circle back with the prominent figures from your internship.
- Call on each of your existing contacts.
- Cast a wider net in your pursuits.
- Relay your resolve to everyone you approach.

Chapter 4
Interview Effectively

The key to successful interviewing lies in your head. Embarking upon your all-important senior-year auditions with a five-star mental approach unquestionably bolsters the chance of convincing your interrogators of your aptitude and ability to do the job. Although a spotless resume lays the groundwork for success, approaching your interviews with poise, conviction, and a clear-cut vision of yourself flourishing in the upper-tier companies you interview with optimizes your potential to deliver under the broil of the interrogation spotlight and to emerge from your trials with offers in hand.

In order to foster an A-1 mentality and cash in on your interviewing opportunities, engage in a measure of intensive preparation ahead of time. Prior to going head-to-head with any of the top-end screeners on your interviewing schedule, partake in any number of constructive activities that refine your presentation, bolster your knowledge base, and, most importantly, promote a confident, winning disposition that breeds peak interviewing performance.

First and foremost, research each of the entities with whom you are interviewing in thorough detail. Take advantage of the Internet. Explore official company websites, leading news and information webpages, plus any other relevant corners of cyberspace, including online newspapers, magazines, and other sites. Read over traditional print materials, such as company annual reports, brochures, and related firm-sanctioned information stores, as well as other relevant resources that offer firm and sector insight.

Study up on core company product offerings and services, histories, backgrounds, and cultures. Educate yourself on corporate leadership, including chief executive officers, chief financial officers, chairmen of the board, etc. Familiarize yourself with noteworthy events such as a recently announced, blowout quarterly earnings report and accompanying breakout stock price, or a momentous acquisition in recent years that transformed the underlying texture of the business. Lastly, read up on relevant news, for example, newly enacted legislation that profoundly shifts the competitive balance of the industry or a game-changing mega-merger involving two immediate company competitors.

Next, do your homework on the nuances of the particular entry-level opportunities on the table. Brush up on your working knowledge of office responsibilities, day-to-day tasks, travel, and typical workweek hours, particularly if they go beyond the conventional forty-hour standard and require weekend commitment.

After carrying out your due diligence, organize your legwork into a central location. Round up the important company facts and figures and supporting material—e.g., firm data sheets, press releases, and articles—and assemble this information into a tidy hard copy or electronic master file, arranged by company. Prior to meeting with a specific employer for the first time, gather up the appropriate company information bundle from your bureau or hard drive, and simply refresh your memory on its contents.

Once you have cobbled together your research into an orderly chief locale, petition others for additional insight. Consult with your mentor, contacts, acquaintances, and other relevant figures, ideally from your targeted field, and press them for inside scoop. Fortify your rudimentary knowledge gained from public, readily available resources with deeper, behind-the-scenes perspective from seasoned veterans on the front lines of the white-collar arena.

Seek out informational interviewing opportunities. Set up informational interviews with professionals from the businesses on your radar, or at least with those gainfully employed in the field who may offer keen, up-to-date industry- and firm-specific intelligence. In the event you are unable to pin down anyone from your list of interviewing companies for an informational interview, individuals from competing firms represent advantageous resources for you to call on—professionals in the same space as your interviewing firm. Even though they cash their paychecks from a different employer than your interviewing firm, they nonetheless provide superlative insight into your sector. The informational interviewing approach remains a particularly expedient device when approaching top-end professionals with whom you maintain only scant or no prior familiarity, such as a gainfully employed individual from your targeted field referred to you by a shared acquaintance.

Within these encounters, probe your hosts for as much inside information as possible. Seek out first-person perspective above and beyond the skin-deep reconnaissance afforded by cyberspace and the traditional print resources at your disposal. Pursue a deeper understanding of firm-specific matters, such as day-to-day inner company workings, business identities and office cultures, everyday working life, particularly among the entry-level ranks, and employer expectations for fresh post-college enlistments. Also, field input on macro themes, such as prevailing sector trends, gross business strategies going forward, and the respective fit of the main players in the broader industry picture. In addition to serving as an effective vehicle for networking and acclimating yourself to the professional sphere, the informational interviewing setup renders a conducive forum for gleaning first-rate perspective and illumination from established figures in a position to offer more penetrating insight.

I participated in a number of these sit-downs amid my own flight path into the professional world. In pursuit of as much third-party input as possible and mindful of the need to upgrade my exposure to the upper end of the white-collar frontier, I arranged several of these meetings and benefited immensely as a result. I even lined up a number of them with professionals from the very entities on my senior-year interviewing docket. (After scoring first-round interviews with a particular employer, I routinely appealed to acquaintances and combed through my contact list in search of relevant connections to the company in question, a highly profitable strategy when successful.) Ultimately, I emerged from these meetings with a greater appreciation for my sector and the relevant players in the field. I gained an understanding of other relevant details that I would not have otherwise been exposed to. In total, these experiences provided an advantageous informational edge that afforded me a major leg up over my interviewing competition. My participation in informational interviewing gave me the necessary knowledge to successfully navigate the interviewing circuit.

As a general rule of thumb, cover all your bases, and be prepared to discuss multiple issues during your interviews. Try not to squander too much time and energy brushing up on every minute, firm-specific and industry detail; rather, soak up the main data points, and maintain a reasonable degree of understanding about them. Get a fix on the full range of topics that may ultimately come up in conversation, and forestall any risk of arriving for your interviews unprepared.

Top-end firms invariably favor candidates who demonstrate a robust grasp of their businesses. Particularly among distinguished companies that foster demanding, high-intensity workplace environs, employers wish to know that their new hires fully realize what they are getting themselves into.

After acquiring superior perspective via informational interviewing, shift gears and turn your attention to your in-person presentation. Dive into the full spread of books, websites, and other information stores on the finer points of successful interviewing, and educate yourself on the nuts and bolts of proper demeanor, eye contact, physical appearance, and any and all other elements in between.

Although the majority of these resources—or at least those worth their salt—lay out their instruction in fine fashion, I nonetheless wish to add my own two cents to the standard fare on one topic in particular. Each of the textbook materials you come into contact with, not to mention outside voices that weigh in, rightly harp on the sheer and utter necessity of employing first-rate eye contact with your interviewers, or any other face-to-face dealings you have along your journey, for that matter. While I whole-heartedly agree, I submit the caveat that *natural* eye contact is key.

Engage your interrogators, or anyone else you interact with, in a comfortable air, such as new contacts you meet with face-to-face for the first time. Avert no eyeballs, and, on the flip side, refrain from holding your gaze on your interviewer's pupils to an excessive degree. That is, steer clear of sparse eye contact, but also do not stare anyone down or go for wide-eyed, over-the-top, eye-to-eye accord 100 percent of the time. Discover a healthy middle ground, and carry on in a loose, instinctive manner. Maintain focus, and, without even thinking about it, allow your eyes to drift off every now and then in spontaneous fashion over the course of conversation. Proper eye contact means confident, unforced, eye-to-eye interface.

I recall a young college intern from my first full-time gig after graduation who missed the mark badly on this important topic. Rather than speak to me, or anyone else in the office for that matter, in a genuine manner, he insisted on boring a hole straight through me every time we spoke. Trying too hard to make an impression, this wide-eyed tenderfoot locked onto my eyes during every one of our face-to-face exchanges as though he were taking part in some type of intense stare-down competition (how he found his way into my employer with that type of hitch in his behavior I have no idea). Instead of enhancing his presentation and elevating his stock in anyone's eyes, his in-person execution had the opposite effect, coming across as artificial and making for awkward office conversation. Although intelligent and dependable in the workplace, he fell flat in this critical area of nonverbal communication. Despite his strong suits, his lacking interpersonal fluency surely dented his prospects to secure a coveted, long-term offer from the company (he received no such commitment from the firm upon the expiration of his apprenticeship).

I fell into this same trap during my first interviews amid senior-year interviewing season. Overly conscious of my eye contact and misguidedly subscribing to the ill-conceived notion of the more eye contact the better, I fixed my gaze on my interviewers during those initial first-round auditions, which worked to my detriment. Rather than approach those opening trials with a composed demeanor, I forced the issue and ended up with an inordinate, unnatural level of eye contact that damaged my stock in the eyes of my suitors. Needless to say, I emerged from these early screenings with zero invitations to return for second-round evaluations. This was a painful early lesson to learn after having worked so hard to line up these meetings in the first place. Although I ultimately rectified the fatal flaw, my off-target presentation curbed my ability to put my best put forward and endear myself to those initial cross-examiners. Akin to the green intern depicted above, my shortcoming thwarted my ability to curry favor with these early interviewers.

After picking up the broader points from the range of online and traditional print materials at your fingertips, embark upon mock interviews. Participate in simulated interviewing sessions with qualified third parties, and further refine your interviewing prowess.

Sign up for such guidance at your university. Contact your campus career services center, and put your name on the list for these training sessions with campus staff tasked with simulating real-life corporate screeners and running you through staged versions of the interviewing wringer. Take advantage of this opportunity to sharpen your interviewing dexterity within this educational, risk-free framework afforded by your campus enrollment. The lion's share of universities make such services available to all of their currently enrolled students; all you have to do is sign up.

Approach these practice flights with the proper frame of mind. In order to get the most out of the experience and elicit candid, constructive feedback, venture forth as though you are going toe-to-toe with the real-life interviewers on your schedule and that your post-college future hangs in the balance. Rehearse your presentation ahead of time, and come up with sharp, pre-scripted inquiries. Arrive on time wearing the appropriate, noncasual business attire. Upon kick off, show yourself well, and aim for a five-star interviewing performance. Put your preparation and training to use, and knock the socks off your interviewers with your poise, dexterity, and precision, just as you would with any top-end suitors for your services.

After testing out the waters within these get-your-feet-wet practice sessions, fully heed the constructive criticisms you receive. Recruit your mentor to weigh in and filter through the incoming commentary and advisement. Incorporate the relevant feedback into your act going forward, even when embarking upon additional simulated interviewing sessions. For example, if a fill-in evaluator calls for greater eye contact and more personality, and your mentor agrees with such counsel, tweak your execution accordingly. Enter into your subsequent interviews, be they simulated or real, with conviction, robust eye contact, and improved punch in your delivery—even when wading into other mock interviews. Take part in as many of these trial runs on your campus as necessary until you have worked out the initial kinks, grown more comfortable with the interviewing construct, and sufficiently readied yourself for the next step in your development.

Although general in nature and not necessarily geared towards any one specific sector—owing to their quarterbacking by academic-centric figures removed from the business arena—these reenactments of the interviewing meat grinder offer a constructive means to ramp up your interviewing skill set, particularly before dipping your toes into the shark-infested big league interviewing waters.

I entered into a pocketful of these on-campus dress rehearsals near the outset of my senior year. Seeking to refine my game before taking on any big dogs from the real-deal corporate world, I took full advantage of this campus resource and picked up perspective that bolstered my interviewing skill set and built up my confidence. Within these engagements, my university-appointed interviewing substitutes flagged holes in my game and sharpened my overall effectiveness. They volunteered frank, colorful observation on everything from my demeanor to the content of my sales pitch to my physical appearance (one in particular, a brusque, to-the-point older fellow, even suggested that I modify my "boyish" haircut prior to auditioning for any top-end company decision makers). In addition to rounding off my initial rough spots and polishing various aspects of my presentation, this honest outside judgment enhanced my conviction in my ability to please the discriminating corporate screeners in my future. These trial runs served as a great introduction to the interviewing process.

Next, implore your mentor to don the surrogate interviewer hat and size up your execution firsthand. Akin to the above, retain your coach to recreate the interviewing pressure cooker and cross-examine you in the style of a veritable corporate evaluator. For best results, set out to make an impression, and treat these mentor-piloted tune-ups as though they were with the true-to-life, no-nonsense, white-collar doorkeepers on your interview schedule. Given his or her experience and firsthand familiarity with your plight after having weathered the same rocky path once before, your adviser may ramp up the intensity and grill you in a more fiery, in-depth manner than the well-intentioned but potentially hemmed-in team of academics from your school. Embracing the persona of a meticulous human resources employee or a sharp-toothed company higher-up remains a difficult task. While mock interviewers on campus can be very effective at helping to prepare you for the future real interviews, they may offer relatively generic scenarios. Your mentor, on the other hand, is likely to possess firsthand context on the inner workings of the professional grid, will be more up to speed on the current business climate, and will be in a better position to conduct a more on-point mock interview.

I called on my mentor to chip in and gauge my prowess in the same manner after trying on the mock interviewing courtesies at my school. My coach picked up the baton from my proxy campus interviewers and seized the reins, subjecting me to an exacting brand of cross-examination on par with my future, real-life corporate screenings. In contrast to the paint-by-number evaluators from my campus, my adviser played the role of tough corporate filter in an Academy Award-worthy performance, running me through the interviewing machine in a vein more reflective of the challenge I faced. Sufficiently versed in my sector after working at one of the same firms on my interviewing schedule, my coach turned up the heat and challenged me with a direct, uncompromising line of interviewing ferocity along the lines of the most inhospitable corporate interrogators on my upcoming interview agenda. Painting an accurate picture of the road ahead, he enlightened me on the particular cadence of my forthcoming screenings and acclimated me to the level of interviewing swelter that awaited. He hardened my resolve, expedited my fine-tuning, and prepared me for life under the interrogation spotlight.

Third, draft others to further augment your mock interviewing education. Recruit the services of gainfully employed contacts and acquaintances, ideally from your targeted sector that know the drill all too well, to submit you to additional grilling and run you through subsequent simulated interviewing sessions. Ideally, these individuals will have been involved in corporate recruiting efforts for their companies and interviewed incoming undergraduate candidates themselves. Inviting more cooks into the kitchen adds another layer of cultivation to the equation and obviously opens you up to more diverse judgment. Enlist these additional experts to bear witness to your presentation as needed until you have polished your delivery and sufficiently readied yourself for live-game action. Bringing in additional external support only aids your cause.

Lastly, take advantage of the second-string interviews on your calendar. Rather than take such meetings lightly and approach them in anything less than a hearty manner, or approach them with a view that they have nothing to offer (or cancel them altogether), embark upon these second-choice screenings in sincere fashion. Show yourself well, just as you would with any top-shelf businesses, and treat these meetings as warm-ups of sorts for your tier-one appointments. Moreover, enter into these engagements with an open mind. Even though you are the one under the microscope, give your hosts every opportunity to sow a favorable impression and sell you on their brands. Furthermore, aim to emerge from such meetings with an offer in hand. Unless the firm behind the offer is significantly below your standards, your procurement of such concrete interest in your services only heightens your appeal to other hiring businesses.

That is not to say you should seek out interviews with less desirable employers in any sort of deceitful fashion— i.e., arranging screenings with lower-priority employers solely as a means of sharpening your skills. Seek no appointments with employers that you maintain absolutely no designs of signing on with after graduation. Rather, schedule any such stops along your senior-year interviewing tour in an optimal sequence. Instead of booking them arbitrarily or interspersed among your tier-one auditions, line up your less-coveted interviews amid the beginning stages of your campaign. Your interviewing talents towards the latter portion of senior-year interviewing season are sure to outshine your skills at the start of your adventure.

While a topflight resume and a refined interviewing skill set undoubtedly bolster your prospects for success, harboring complete and total confidence surpasses all. Hazarding upon your cardinal undergraduate interviews with unshakable self-assuredness spells your best chance to distinguish yourself from the interviewing competition and to charm your way into an esteemed corporate domain. If you genuinely believe you have what it takes, you give yourself the best opportunity to seed a decisively favorable impression with choosy corporate screeners. Self-possession and a cool demeanor unquestionably foster the best impression and breed peak interviewing performance.

Pore over your educational materials, and sit down with your mentor and others to hone your craft, but, most importantly, partake in intensive preparation and training in order to cultivate superlative interviewing confidence.

During my second full year of post-graduation employment, once I had earned the unofficial title of "senior analyst" in my group, I chipped in to my employer's broader recruiting wheel on occasion and conducted interviews with a number of undergraduate hopefuls vying for entrance into the firm. Of all the first-year prospects I sat down with, one individual in particular stood out high above the pack, oozing total confidence. In addition to wielding a compelling resume and demonstrating a firm grasp of the sector, this standout candidate fended off my curveballs with ease and breezed through the inquisition like a champ. Without coming across as overly presumptuous or pompous, he conveyed his readiness for the job and made it abundantly clear that he knew what he was getting himself into. In the simplest of terms, he had "it."

Needless to say, upon reporting back to my higher-ups, I cast a firm vote in his favor. Sharing my sentiment after wrapping up their own evaluations of him, my superiors, fearful of losing out on his first-rate talents to another firm, quickly pounced, offering him a formal invitation to join our esteemed company prior to his even exiting the building that day.

I clearly recall my own finest interviewing hour as a bright-eyed graduating college senior in more or less the same position less than two years earlier. After shuffling through a stretch of lackluster showings amid the early stages of my campaign and suffering the attendant crush of rejection, I finally righted my ship. (In hindsight, I realize that I had tried too hard and forced the issue in those early trials, which unsurprisingly ended in failure.) Prior to entering into a much-anticipated series of day-long, final round interviews with a top-of-the-line employer up next on the docket, I realized that I had absolutely nothing to lose and only a resplendent future to gain. At that defining moment, I made up my mind to reel in my nerves and permit the full range of my self-assuredness to flow forth. I remained up for the task, as I had sufficiently prepared myself for my all-important trials and it was simply a matter of putting it all together and driving that message home to these corporate evaluators. Upon arriving for show time, I unleashed my confidence full force and proceeded to enter "the zone." Brimming with newfound poise and composure, I handled all interrogator inquiries with finesse and passed all tests with flying colors. Once the dust had settled, I finally netted my first five-star offer of full-time employment.

Only after self-assessing and unleashing my inner juice did I finally arrive. Although I had previously rehearsed my routine and had sufficiently educated myself on the interviewing road ahead, it was only after shedding my early stiffness, demonstrating genuine inner belief, and displaying a true sense of belonging with the high-octane corporate environment and the firms hosting me for interview that I finally broke through and earned my way into coveted full-time employment with a topflight firm.

Action Items for Chapter 4: Interview Effectively

- Prepare ahead of time.
- Research each of the firms on your interviewing docket in thorough detail.
- Organize your legwork into a central location.
- Consult with your mentor, close contacts, and acquaintances from your targeted field. Petition others for additional insight.
- Seek out informational interviews.
- Sharpen your in-person presentation. Be punctual, and wear the appropriate attire.
- Dive into books, websites, and other relevant information stores.
- Embark on mock interviews.
- Rehearse your presentation ahead of time.

Chapter 5
Craft a Superior Resume

Your resume remains a critical ingredient to your success. A concise, comprehensive portrait of your four-year undergraduate track record, this crucial piece of the job-search puzzle serves as your primary means, at least initially, to communicate your candidacy to the upper-tier businesses on your radar. Craft a mediocre, pedestrian snapshot of your body of work, and you will surely sabotage your chances to nail down top-end employment. On the other hand, compose a cohesive, unblemished single-page synopsis that effectively encapsulates your academic achievements, constructive work experience, and involvement in extracurricular activities, and you will convey your aptitude and fitness for the corporate frontier and differentiate yourself from your peers while appeasing an intensely resume-oriented recruiting engine.

Formulate a compelling resume because employers examine incoming entry-level resumes in only cursory fashion. Particularly the higher you aim up the corporate food chain, firms pass snap judgment and cast the die on the interviewing fates of undergraduate employment hopefuls in a matter of nanoseconds, assuming they even take the time to read over their resumes in the first place. Prior to your even gaining the opportunity to showcase your skill set to any company hiring managers or human resources personnel over the telephone or in person, your candidacy on paper unquestionably imparts an indelible impression in the minds of the corporate gatekeepers who receive it. Your fitness for the professional world and your post-diploma future are determined in a heartbeat, solely on the basis of the subject matter you have crafted into a single confining sheet of resume paper.

Furthermore, your resume remains center stage even after you have cleared the initial corporate filter. After gaining entrance into the interviewing mill, your one-pager, with rare exception, sets a critical early tone and serves as a focal point for your all-important cross-examinations. Even in instances where you successfully lock down interviewing privileges via credible third-party endorsement and seemingly secure an early lead over your interviewing competition, your resume stands front and center. Despite having a recommendation, you bear the burden of marketing your skill set and giving off the best impression, beginning with your presentation on paper. Your resume remains a prime focal point with all manner of interviewers.

Certain interviewers open their screenings by requesting that you "walk them through your resume." In this case, you simply run through your full undergraduate narrative in descriptive but concise fashion, starting at the top and working your way down as laid out in your summation.

Other inquisitors treat your one-pager as an itinerary of sorts. Rather than defer to you to recount your achievements and experiences of the prior four years, these individuals pore over your qualifications with a meticulous eye and pepper you with challenging questions as they make their way through your resume.

Another type of interrogator welcomes you into their office under a chilly air, opening the proceedings under a shroud of uncomfortable silence as they acquaint themselves with your credentials. Preoccupied with your resume rather than the individual before them, at least at the start, these off-putting personalities leave you in anxious solitude as they get up to speed on your history at their own exacting pace, much to your discomfort and agitation, before engaging you any further. Mid-level and senior, non-HR employees commonly conduct their interrogations in such a way, reviewing the merits of your candidacy for the first time during the interview. Bogged down by their regular office functions, these higher-up-the-totem busy bees bear precious little time to sift through incoming applications, particularly those of undergraduates.

Although certainly not the only one, I encountered one individual in particular who fit this description to a T during final-round interviews with a prominent investment bank amid one of my employment-scouting excursions to New York. Upon arriving on the scene to market my wares, I came face-to-face with a gruff, no-nonsense managing director with absolutely no time for pleasantries. After entering his office, introducing myself, and taking my seat on the other side of his executive desk, I sat in virtual silence for a stretch, with beads of sweat brimming to the surface, while this intimidating senior professional painstakingly gave my resume a thorough once-over, obviously for the first time. After a few muted, painful minutes, he promptly launched into full-on, bulldog investigator mode and grilled me on various aspects of my composition. Keeping the temperature dial turned up, he nitpicked my responses and probed into the finer points of my presentation, questioning my highlights and decision making at every turn. At one point, this thorn in my side even challenged me on my knowledge of one of the personal hobbies I had listed.

Lastly, a rare breed of interviewer introduces himself or herself politely enough and engages you in casual conversation as they take in your resume. However, rather than make such a close study of your work and grill you with precise questions or come at you with absurd brain teasers or riddles while they size up your reaction, these harmless figures bring out your personality and aim to get to know you on a personal level. Although aware of your presentation on paper, this refreshing strain of corporate interrogator harps on your resume the least relative to the other, more exasperating cross-examiners on your interviewing docket. However, despite the civil veneer, do not mistake their hospitality and lack of interviewing combustion for a dearth of attentiveness to your one-pager. Despite appearances to the contrary and their easygoing personality, your resume no doubt remains under the microscope.

I recall meeting one such character in particular who fell into this last category of interviewer, offering only scant surface attention to my resume. In contrast to my other interviewing adversaries, this affable figure spent the better part of our meeting engaging me in cordial fashion, posing resume-centric questions only intermittently. A junior member of the company workforce not much older than I was, he seemed more interested in talking about sports, our personal backgrounds, college life, and other such off-subject topics. Although I appreciated the display of humanity and tried hard to relay an agreeable personality, while at the same time convincing him of my ability to do the job, I knew better than to let my guard down too much and misconstrue his seeming indifference to my qualifications for a lack of interest in my resume. Despite his disarming style, there was no question he had thoroughly sized up my resume.

Furthermore, your late-stage interviewers may raise the bar. In order to pare down their prospect lists and weed out any unfit applicants, your second-round cross-examiners and beyond may up the ante and hold you and your resume to a higher standard relative to the first barrier of resume screeners who authorized your passage onto the interviewing conveyor belt in the first place. (Human resources personnel commonly handle the initial screening process, particularly at the junior levels of the workforce. In my situation, I met with a mid-level human resources employee for my very first interview with my eventual first post-graduation employer.) You require a solid resume to make the cut and successfully navigate the entire interviewing machine.

Virtually all of my interviewers picked my resume to the bone. With rare exception, each and every corporate interrogator seated across from me pored over my one-pager with a fine-tooth comb. Not wishing to unfurl the company welcome mat to just anyone, the bulk of these evaluators took a long, hard look at my document, dissecting it line-by-line, while the rest zeroed in on only certain aspects of my presentation and fired off their questions accordingly. Needless to say, I required an A+ resume to survive the heavy scrutiny. I needed a quality presentation on paper to kick off my screenings on a favorable note and pave the way for fluid dialogue with my interviewers. Irrespective of my interviewing skill set, venturing into my interviews with a flawed presentation in any way surely would have transmitted a less-than-robust signal and grounded my ability to perform under the cross-examination, assuming I even earned the green light to interview in the first place. Any blemishes or shortcomings within my document surely would have had nowhere to hide. My capacity to charm my interviewers and steer my post-college fate hinged profoundly on the caliber of my resume.

In order to fashion a superior document that introduces your credentials in fine fashion and implants a decisively favorable perception of your candidacy in the minds of hiring managers, adhere to a comprehensive plan of attack. Implement an ambitious, multifaceted formula for success in which you refine your resume over the course of several stages until emerging with an astute, well-constructed formulation that lays the groundwork for interviewing success and paves the way to choice, career-flowering employment.

Prior to putting pen to page and commencing construction on your all-important creation, engage in an intensive measure of preparation and research. Investigate the deluge of readily available instructional materials on effective resume writing. Explore the range of information at your campus career services center, comb through the Internet, and devour books, articles, and other relevant materials on the topic. Supplement your textbook refinement with hands-on instructional workshops or clinics available on or off campus, such as fee-based services provided by private, third-party educators outside of your academic institution. Take full advantage of the full sweep of resources readily available in cyberspace and on bookshelves, and sign up for instructor-piloted guidance to enhance your knowledge of proper resume construction.

Once you have acquainted yourself with the full spread of resources at your disposal, seek out the real-life resumes of actual students. Top off your textbook and tutor-led training, and round up a sampling of model one-pagers from top-tier undergraduates from prior years, ideally within your targeted field, who translated their touchstone presentations on paper into gainful employment.

That is not to say you should overlook any blue-chip works authored by graduates who majored in different areas or landed first-rate jobs outside of your post-college area of interest. Given the scarcity of such presentations and relative difficulty in obtaining them, take note of any other five-star one-pagers you come across, and incorporate any inspiring elements into your own offering. Make use of any quality documents worth emulating from areas outside of your preferred post-graduation field.

Consult with your mentor, contacts, peers, and any other pertinent parties who may direct you to any such pearls of resume composition. Perhaps an established elder professional from your favored sector may drum up a smattering of resumes from his circle of successful colleagues. Or a higher-up from your undergraduate internship may scare up a batch from his employer, with, of course, the proper permission or entirely scrubbed of any personal data such as name, address, telephone number, etc.

An important note: always procure such pieces of work in ethical fashion. Respect the privacy of others, and never assume possession of anyone else's personal property or information by improper or unlawful means. Ensure you have secured the proper authorization or approval, and take care that any individuals assisting you in the process have also acted accordingly.

In the waning days of spring during my first full year of employment after college, my employer enlisted a fresh crop of business school students—Master of Business Administration students in between their first and second years of business school—into its summer MBA internship program. Filtering in from an impressive collection of premier academic institutions across the nation, each of these temporary additions to the firm, upon arrival for orientation, received a warm corporate welcome. They also received a freshly minted copy of the accompanying information package outlining the itinerary and other aspects of their tour of duty with my employer. Most notably, this spruce company packet contained an appendix of the uncut resumes of each of the participants in the summer-long affair, all of whom were cream-of-the-crop and had top quality credentials. (Like the undergraduate internships, the standout performers, in addition to gaining indispensable resume filler and experience, also fielded desirable long-term offers of employment from the company at summer's end.) Needless to say, minimal time passed before this juicy article of interest had made the rounds in my corner of the firm, particularly among the curious junior-level ranks. I came across a copy of this intriguing nugget as soon as two conscripts from the program reported for duty in my group at the start of that summer.

This collection of masterworks embodied quintessential resume composition. Although not intended for personal use outside the firm (our human resources staff had surely designed the circular with only internal consumption in mind), a number of copies floated around and some inevitably made their way into the hands of non-employees. This slice of model formulations clearly represented an absolute gold mine of a resource for ambitious graduating university seniors, or any other aspiring second-year business school students, for that matter, aiming to cook up a formidable resume and vie for high-reaching full-time employment.

Perhaps an enlistee from the program may lend out his copy. With the necessary approval and after wiping all immaterial personal details, perhaps a summer business school associate may, in lawful fashion, of course, bestow his booklet of gold standard resumes to a deserving soon-to-be-graduate in need of assistance.

The actual formulations of topflight, real-life college students from prior years represent your best roadmaps to success, particularly in comparison to the sample resumes offered up in your academic resources.

After educating yourself on the principles of dynamic resume construction and cobbling together an acceptable allotment of model resumes, break ground on your first draft. Using your masterworks, or perhaps a single touchstone presentation in particular for inspiration, craft your full inventory of achievements and experiences of the past four years into a convincing preliminary formulation.

Although a full-on resume discussion lies beyond the scope of this book, and I have no intention of reinventing the wheel or regurgitating the endless volume of material already penned on the subject, I offer up my own two cents in the pages that follow.

Format. You need not necessarily conform to a specific, one-size-fits-all template, but operate within effective resume-building parameters nevertheless. Even though you harbor ample leeway in terms of the mold you ultimately employ—certainly no two resumes are exactly alike—comply with proper resume protocol, and lay out your one-pager in a fluid, aesthetically appealing framework devoid of any eccentricities or unseemly features that draw negative attention or raise red flags with employers. Present your four-year track record in optimal packaging.

Reproduce the rhythm and flow of your model resumes, and arrange the key elements of your creation in accordance with your level of seasoning (or lack thereof). Place your university and academic highlights at the beginning of your document—but immediately beneath your contact information: name, home address, primary telephone number, e-mail address, etc.—and detail your internship and work experience just below. Then, include any personal data points of note at the bottom, for example, any relevant computer skills, second language proficiencies, hobbies, and other interests. Lastly, consider adding the phrase "References available upon request."

Employers regard academics and, to a lesser degree, work experience, above all else, depending on your particular circumstances. These two core pieces of the puzzle represent your chief selling points and therefore comprise the sum and substance of your presentation.

Appearance. Create the impression that a single sheet of resume paper can hardly contain your abundance of scholastic achievement, quality work experience, and robust involvement in extracurricular activities, plus any other relevant skill sets, hobbies, or other personal interests you wish to note. Sow the perception that if your resume could muster a voice, it would speak at length on your surplus of undergraduate accolades and experiences.

Exploit the full expanse of paper real estate at your disposal. Without compromising the caliber of your content with unnecessary wordiness or hollow filler, load up your page with your accomplishments in a concise, illustrative fashion that minimizes the appearance of excess white or empty space in your document. Paint the portrait of a diligent, goal-oriented candidate awash in production and achievement.

Resume A

John A. Doe
1234 Any Street Drive
Any City, ST 12345
(123) 456-7890
Johnadoe@Johnadoe.com

EDUCATION

Big Name University
Huge Name School of Business

Any City, ST
May 2016

- Bachelor of Business Administration, GPA 3.75/4.00
- Dean's List (4 times)
- Prominent Name Honor Transfer Scholarship recipient
- XYZ Fellowship for Scholastic Excellence Award
- President of ABC Business Management Honor Society
- Class Representative for Student Executive Board of Trustees
- Treasurer of Finance Club

WORK EXPERIENCE

Great Time Airlines, Inc.
Financial Analyst Intern

Any City, ST
September 2015 – January 2016

- Performed annual expense planning and headcount plus salary development for company Top Shelf Clubs, Mileage Miler Program and Luxury Lounge for continental Europe and domestic Northwest
- Compiled applicable financial data and guest information into company Allocation Inquiries in support of various club refurbishment projects
- Managed station and department budgeting; worked closely with station management to devise yearly spending and headcount plans
- Oversaw newly implemented market-based revenue plan - devised cargo revenue for western division and adjusted plan quarterly to reflect market fluctuations
- Developed profit & loss analysis for new and existent terminal stations and presented monthly station profitability results to upper management and station management

Any Name Securities Co.
Fixed Income Intern

Any City, ST
June 2015 – August 2015

- Developed profit & loss analysis to accurately track results for mortgage security trading desk
- Executed financial models, industry market research, analysis, and valuation for significant client securities offering
- Processed client account forms for distribution to company's west coast office in accordance with XYZ regulations

Fancy Name Company Ltd.
Office Manager

Any City, ST
September 2014 – May 2015

- Trained new employees for corporate office, maintained employee work schedules, and managed payroll adjustments
- Managed corporate accounts receivable and accounts payable

Professional Sports Team
Marketing Intern

Any City, ST
November 2013 – February 2014

- Aided marketing department with 2014 All-Star Game voting process
- Coordinated with co-workers and fellow interns to produce creative team regalia for fan use during home games

ADDITIONAL INFORMATION

Computer skills: Microsoft Excel, PowerPoint, Word, Bloomberg, Reuters
Language proficiency: fluent in Spanish, knowledge of French
Personal interests: sports, outdoor activities, movies, travel, art

References available upon request

Resume B

John A. Doe
1234 Any Street Drive
Any City, ST 12345
(123) 456-7890
Johnadoe@Johnadoe.com

EDUCATION

Big Name University   Any City, ST
Huge Name School of Business   May 2016

- Bachelor of Business Administration, GPA 3.75/4.00

- Dean's List

- Treasurer of Finance Club

WORK EXPERIENCE

Great Time Airlines, Inc.   Any City, ST
Financial Analyst Intern   September 2015 – January 2016

- Performed annual expense planning and salary development for company Top Shelf Clubs, Mileage Miler Program and Luxury Lounge

- Compiled applicable financial data and guest information into company Allocation Inquiries

Any Name Securities Co.   Any City, ST
Fixed Income Intern   June 2015 – August 2015

- Developed profit & loss analysis to track results for mortgage security trading desk

- Executed financial models, industry market research, and valuation for client

Fancy Name Company Ltd.   Any City, ST
Office Manager   September 2014 – May 2015

- Trained new employees for corporate office, maintained employee work schedules, and managed payroll adjustments

- Managed corporate accounts receivable and accounts payable

ADDITIONAL INFORMATION

Computer skills (Microsoft Office), knowledge of Spanish, personal interests include: sports, outdoor activities, movies, travel, art

Examine the first two resumes depicted (Resume A and Resume B). What is your first reaction? Which formulation do you prefer at first glance? Resume A clearly appears to be the more astutely constituted production of the two and seems to have been contrived by an upper-tier candidate. Resume B, on the other hand, lacks density in comparison and looks as though it were crafted by a pedestrian or inferior prospect. Resume B registers nothing on the "wow" factor scale, whereas Resume A bursts with substance, particularly when stacked up against its skimpy counterpart. As a result of its livelier appearance and richer surface appeal, Resume A easily takes the cake in this comparison. If Resume B ultimately comprises the superior content of the two, its author has committed the cardinal sin of selling his candidacy short and failing to present his credentials in optimal fashion.

Take advantage of the formatting tools at your disposal. To achieve the desired effect and take your presentation up a notch, adjust your layout. Tailor your synopsis to fit your robust body of work, and squeeze your information into a single page via the use of two formatting devices in your toolkit, particularly if your content spills over to a second page and you have no excess fat to trim. Recalibrate your margins first and foremost. Without going too far and detracting from your quality, expand your margins both horizontally and vertically. You certainly need not confine yourself to the preset default margins in your word processor application. Additionally, reduce your font size, if necessary. If you need more room to operate and have enough leeway to effect such a move without compromising your configuration, take your script down by a fraction, provided there is room to drop down further and such an adjustment keeps you in accordance with the axioms of proper resume construction protocol and does not force your readers to pull out a magnifying lens to decipher your subject matter.

Resume C

John A. Doe
1234 Any Street Drive
Any City, ST 12345
(123) 456-7890
Johnadoe@Johnadoe.com

EDUCATION

Big Name University — Any City, ST
Huge Name School of Business — May 2016
- Bachelor of Business Administration, GPA 3.75/4.00
- Dean's List (4 times)
- Prominent Name Honor Transfer Scholarship recipient
- XYZ Fellowship for Scholastic Excellence Award
- President of ABC Business Management Honor Society
- Class Representative for Student Executive Board of Trustees
- Treasurer of Finance Club

WORK EXPERIENCE

Great Time Airlines, Inc. — Any City, ST
Financial Analyst Intern — September 2015 – January 2016
- Performed annual expense planning and headcount plus salary development for company Top Shelf Clubs, Mileage Miler Program and Luxury Lounge for continental Europe and domestic Northwest
- Compiled applicable financial data and guest information into company Allocation Inquiries in support of various club refurbishment projects
- Managed station and department budgeting; worked closely with station management to devise yearly spending and headcount plans
- Performed monthly closing duties, researched and illustrated variances versus plan, reclassed headcount, compiled divisional profit & loss book for presentation to departmental vice president
- Oversaw newly implemented market-based revenue plan - devised cargo revenue for western division and adjusted plan quarterly to reflect market fluctuations
- Developed profit & loss analysis for new and existent terminal stations and presented monthly station profitability results to upper management and station management

Any Name Securities Co. — Any City, ST
Fixed Income Intern — June 2015 – August 2015
- Developed profit & loss analysis to accurately track results for mortgage security trading desk
- Executed financial models, industry market research, analysis, and valuation for significant client securities offering
- Processed client account forms for distribution to company's west coast office in accordance with XYZ regulations

Fancy Name Company Ltd. — Any City, ST
Office Manager — September 2014 – May 2015
- Trained new employees for corporate office, maintained employee work schedules, and managed payroll adjustments
- Arranged monthly client payment schedules and coordinated with clients to arrange due payments
- Managed corporate accounts receivable and accounts payable

Professional Sports Team — Any City, ST
Marketing Intern — November 2013 – February 2014
- Aided marketing department with 2014 All-Star Game voting process
- Coordinated with co-workers and fellow interns to produce creative team regalia for fan use during home games

ADDITIONAL INFORMATION

Computer skills: Microsoft Excel, PowerPoint, Word, Bloomberg, Reuters
Language proficiency: fluent in Spanish, knowledge of French
Personal interests: sports, outdoor activities, movies, travel, art

References available upon request

Note that in Resume C, by expanding your margins, you beef up your presentation that much more. By taking up additional—but not too much—space in such fashion, you further sow the perception of a topflight candidate laden with production. Your final resume appears even more robust.

Outward aesthetics obviously matters profoundly. Content aside, surface charm shapes our perceptions immensely. In the example, we formulate indelible impressions of the resumes depicted in the blink of an eye and pass firm judgment on the aptitude of the underlying architects. Obviously, employers do the same.

Craft your work in the manner of Resume C. Fashion your body of work such that if it were inserted into the equation alongside Resumes A, B, and C—again, excluding content for the moment—it would much more closely resemble the opulence of Resume C. Pass the surface appeal litmus test with flying colors, and look the part of a topflight hopeful flush with polish and execution.

Bullet Points. Employ crisp bullet points. Expound upon your academic history and pre-graduation seasoning in the professional arena with succinct, well-crafted bullets or supporting text. Utilize polished resume lexicon devoid of unrefined, colloquial, or bland language that is neither overly concise, in the manner of Resume B, or, on the flip side, exceedingly wordy. Strike a fine balance between the two, and craft your subject matter in a fashion that demonstrates competence and professionalism.

Consider the following example:

- Helped bosses with time-consuming order entry of worker hours and also wrote down all of their successes or failures

Overly short and devoid of exemplary English, this under-whelming delineation clearly bears room for improvement.

Now consider the following entry:

- Managed entire full-time employee work schedule database and regularly updated daily performance log of all hourly company personnel on behalf of immediate superiors and other upper management

This second configuration clearly represents an upgrade. The sharpened language bolsters the overall quality of the bullet point and more effectively conveys the tasks performed. The souped-up content packs more punch and improves overall surface appeal.

Tighten up any low-grade or unpolished prose, and fortify your content with sharp detail. Fashion your subject matter in a grain that optimizes your presentation and manifests five-star aptitude.

Well-roundedness. Portray a diligent, well-balanced student with no use for idle, unproductive time. Cap your academic highlights and pre-graduation work history with a full rundown of your involvement in constructive extra-curricular activities. Name off your memberships in campus clubs, honors societies, sororities or fraternities, university-sanctioned or intramural athletic endeavors, humanitarian or charitable pursuits, student government, and any other dynamic on- or off-campus undertakings that merit inclusion in your resume. Omit any partisan, extreme-leaning, or other potentially controversial associations that may drive a wedge between yourself and potential employers, such as any radioactive religious or party-specific political affiliations. Wrap up your resume with noteworthy personal skill sets—e.g., computer proficiencies, foreign language fluencies, etc.—followed by any interesting hobbies and lei-sure activities, including travel, reading, sports, and music, that offer a glimpse into your personal side and may pique the interest of interviewers.

Amid my second year of full-time employment after graduation, two bright college interns arrived on the scene to apprentice in my group as part of the firm's summer under-graduate internship program. Although both newcomers impressed on paper, one in particular wielded an absolute gem of a resume. This smashing young dynamo had attended her university on a full academic ride, clawed out a spotless grade point average, boasted numerous awards and accolades for academic excellence, interned with a top management consulting firm prior to coming on board with my employer, and, to top it off, sported a vibrant ledger of extracurricular involvements. Furthermore, she had travelled the globe extensively, featured first-rate computer skills, spoke two distinct languages outside of her native tongue, and owned a slew of other intriguing talents and personal interests (how she found time for all these impressive things, I have no idea). Although her academic institution lacked eye-popping, name-brand recognition, truth be told, her presentation on paper clearly depicted an all-around impressive, star-quality young lady.

Unsurprisingly, not long after winding down her tour of duty with my employer, returning to school to finish her degree, and subsequently embarking on her big-league, senior-year interviews, she bagged a highly coveted offer of post-college employment from the number-one investment banking house on Wall Street, a solid gold opportunity that she promptly accepted. Despite her non-Ivy League pedigree, her unrivaled well-roundedness distinguished her from even her most decorated peers. Her diversity and dizzying range of interests and accomplishments eclipsed virtually every other undergraduate resume I encountered.

Employers unquestionably look for versatility in new entry-level recruits. In addition to farming for prowess within the classroom and favorable pre-graduation exposure to the professional arena, company hiring managers revere multidimensional candidates who demonstrate a capacity to interact well with others and make solid use of their time.

Illustrate your multifaceted qualities, and "check the box." Satisfy all employer preconditions for employment hopefuls in your position. Forestall the raising of any red flags with company hiring managers, and fully satisfy their criteria for fresh undergraduate additions to their workforces. Portray yourself as a dynamic, all-purpose candidate with sturdy credentials, multiple skills, and a brimming ledger of personal involvements.

Leadership

Relay your ability to lead. Communicate your predisposition to captain your endeavors and take on prominent roles in your undertakings. Highlight any officer positions or any specific titles of note you held within the clubs, organizations, and pursuits, on or off campus that you claim membership in, such as president, vice president, secretary, treasurer, etc. Also, note other principal or authoritative hats you wore, such as captain of your college baseball team, organizer of a campus billiards club, founder of your local chapter of a nationwide honors society specific to your area of study, chairman of your University Student Affairs committee, etc. Specify any front-row capacities you shouldered over the course of your undergraduate tenure that showcase your enterprise and literacy in leadership.

Moreover, foster a proactive theme throughout the body of your document. Compose in a track that projects an aura of forefront involvement in your experiences. When expounding upon your role within your internship(s), convey your capacity to bear the torch and assume signal-calling duties and responsibilities. Employ language that characterizes your efforts as actively engaged, and, at the same time, eliminate verbiage that suggest passivity or a lack of assertiveness on your part. Convey your ability to adopt frontline roles.

Refer back to the sample bullet points on page 148. Recall my reconfiguration of "Helped bosses with time-consuming order entry of worker hours and also wrote down all of their successes or failures" into the more astutely formulated and more leadership-evoking "Managed entire full-time employee work schedule database and regularly updated daily performance log of all hourly company personnel on behalf of immediate superiors and other upper management." In addition to elevating the caliber of the content, note that I deliberately swapped out the more recessive "helped"—a potential undersell of your contributions—in favor of the more commanding "managed." This simple improvement in word choice upgrades outside perception of your tasks performed. Utilize more potent language wherever able, and optimize the portrayal of your experiences—e.g., *managed, organized, spearheaded, executed* rather than *helped, assisted, supported.*

Employers cherish leadership and initiative within any new conscripts they bring aboard. Upper-tier companies invariably opt for fearless personalities who seize the reins of their undertakings and display an inclination to take on weighty or principal roles in the groups they join and the projects they undertake. Hiring firms shy away from candidates who come across as deferential and suggest a pattern of waiting for others to call the shots rather than getting out in front and directing traffic themselves. Businesses remain loathe to hire hopefuls who exhibit minimal or no inclination for leadership, show a reluctance to pilot their affairs, and appear content to remain simple spokes in the wheels of their ventures. Employers want leaders, not followers.

Once you assemble a cohesive preliminary draft, recruit others to pitch in and fine-tune your work, just as you did to ramp up your interviewing skill set. Call on your mentor to chip in and size up your first take—given her proximity to your efforts thus far, she should suggest only nominal changes at this point. After reflecting any necessary adjustments, return to her with an updated version for another run-through, particularly if she had significant corrections or suggestions. Repeat this process of integrating her changes and resubmitting your work to her as many times as necessary until she has signed off on your last draft and you have emerged with a more refined composition.

After consulting with your mentor and chiseling out a near-finished product, enlist additional individuals to weigh in. Call on competent third parties to impart further judgment, such as experienced colleagues and acquaintances from the professional sphere familiar with your objectives and fully versed in the nuances of undergraduate resume composition. At this point, you likely require only one or two additional sets of eyes to take further stock of your creation and deliver any final remarks. Once your panel of experts has finished evaluating your work and imparted any closing comments, upload any repairs, with oversight from your mentor, into your last draft. After making the necessary changes and applying the finishing touches—and all parties involved have signed off on your end product—you may finally venture to the printers for a final impression of your work on paper.

In my case, after huddling with my mentor and drawing up a competent configuration, I forwarded my composition to a crew of astute personal acquaintances for further review—in this case, a colleague three years my senior and two close business school cronies of my mentor, all of whom held down frontline posts within the financial services arena, my first-choice destination after graduation. After reviewing their suggestions, I incorporated the necessary modifications with input from my coach and finally emerged from the process with an exquisite, fit-to-print showpiece worthy of dissemination to reputable businesses. Versed in the game after having already been around the block and mastered the art of the resume themselves, these indispensable contributors imparted sage observations and pointed out soft spots in my document that neither I nor my mentor had picked up on previously. These wellsprings of resume expertise brought a fresh perspective that proved to be the final coat of polish I needed to vault my presentation over the top.

You need not necessarily adhere to this particular script to a T, but seek out external assistance, in any event. My suggested approach reflects only one of many potential plans of attack you may put into effect. For example, you may wish to field input from your mentor and various other contributors at the outset, or, although not necessarily my top recommendation, you may wish to consult with only your mentor throughout the process and mold your resume in a fashion similar to his creation. In any event, in order to churn out a crown jewel that rivals the senior-year summations of your most savvy peers, open up your efforts to external scrutiny, and seek out criticism from experienced voices from the professional sphere in position to lend contributive expertise. Graduating college seniors who naively avoid outside support and bypass this crucial step inevitably come up with unimpressive final products that simply fail to measure up in the eyes of discriminating employers. Consulting with others remains a key component of your success. Going at it alone remains one of the worst mistakes you can make.

A note about cover letters

After crafting a compelling resume, compose a first-rate cover letter. A complement to your one-pager, a cover letter introduces you to potential employers and features additional information not necessarily apparent in your resume. This extension of your resume sheds more light on your background, experience, and skill set. Although your resume remains of utmost importance, a well-formulated cover letter bolsters your possibilities to satisfy discriminating company hiring managers.

Pen a cover letter that stands out. Consult the smorgasbord of websites and other resources on the topic for guidance, and engineer a concise composition that effectively expounds upon your credentials, highlights your strengths, delineates your suitability for the position, and telegraphs your interest in the firm, including the reason for your interest.

For best results, adhere to a cohesive formula for success. Akin to quality resume fabrication, employ punch-packing, personal descriptors, such as *enterprising, dependable, detail-oriented*, etc. Moreover, tailor your cover letter to your audience. In other words, utilize different cover letters for different situations. For example, if pursuing a specific employment opportunity, gear your subject matter toward the particular full-time post in question. If submitting your application unsolicited to an enterprise with no express openings for graduating college seniors, and the situation warrants, register your interest with an all-embracing cover letter. If you boast a noteworthy personal referral, name the referring party at the beginning of your letter. Where applicable, direct your offering to a particular individual within the company, such as the human resources employee or company point-person listed in the posting. Lastly, confine your efforts to only one page and three or four paragraphs in length.

Although cover letters are not a necessity for every opportunity you chase down, draw up a sturdy, ready-for-dispatch template at the outset, in any event. When applying for a particular position, determine whether or not adding a cover letter adds value. As a general rule of thumb, err on the side of caution, and submit a cover letter with your appeal. Never deviate from proper convention and attach a cover letter if the listing expressly requests resumes only, and, on the flip side, always include a cover letter if explicitly requested in the job posting.

The best cover letters I ever came across radiated polish. (As I previously discussed, once I established myself and found my footing with my employer, I screened fresh undergraduate prospects on occasion in support of the broader company-recruiting engine.) Well-crafted and incisive, these sparkling gems complied with proper construction protocol on all counts. Furthermore, rather than come across as more of the same dime-a-dozen credentials and unknown names on paper, in the manner of the bulk of the resumes from the broader undergraduate talent pool, these five-star configurations painted the portrait of real, dynamic fireballs that dripped with potential. Leaving a positive impression with me, these superlative showpieces bolstered my confidence in the underlying architects and set the table for constructive interviews. Their mastery on paper shone through and fortified their chances of landing coveted interviews with my employer.

Although not necessarily the most critical ingredient to your success—the majority of resume screeners assess cover letters only after poring over the accompanying resumes, myself included—a concise, professional cover letter further differentiates your candidacy from those of the broader graduating college senior pack.

Action Items for Chapter 5: Craft a Superior Resume

- Engage in an intensive measure of preparation and research.
- Take full advantage of the range of resources at your campus career services center.
- Search the Internet; review articles, books, and other relevant materials.
- Look into hands-on instructional workshops or clinics.
- Seek out real-life resumes as models. Always procure other resumes in ethical fashion.
- Operate within effective resume composition parameters.
- Employ formatting tools to present a robust impression.
- Compose crisp bullet points.
- Convey well-roundedness, an ability to lead, and pro-activeness.
- Recruit others to review and fine-tune your resume.
- Compose a first-rate, one-page cover letter tailored to your audience.

Parting Advice

A im for excellence in all areas. In order to get the most out of your job search and land the brand of post-diploma employment you covet, tone up your gray matter, formulate a crown jewel of a resume, sharpen your interviewing wit, and retain a skillful mentor to ensure your fitness on all fronts.

Do not wade into your job search with any weak links in the chain. If one aspect of your presentation lags, shore up the deficiency in question, and set sail with a balanced attack. For example, if you boast a stellar disposition and a rock-solid resume, but struggle in the interviewing department after trying a few interviews on for size, bring your in-person faculties up to par before engaging any more suitors for your services, particularly those of the upper-tier variety. Embark on more mock and informational interviews. Do everything in your power to sharpen your execution before going any further. Set out on your campaign with every piece of the puzzle firmly in place.

Furthermore, do not count on a particular strong suit to carry the day. For example, if your resume stands out as your chief selling point, do not rely on it to make up for any shortcomings elsewhere. You still have to pursue your opportunities. You still have to perform well during critical interviews. Sharpen the other arrows in your quiver before setting out to conquer the task at hand. Abstain from venturing into your job search with anything but an optimum mental approach, presentation on paper, and interviewing skill set. Hone all aspects of your operation. Bring as much to the table as possible.

Tear into your campaign with unmatched fervor. Interview on your campus extensively. Network, scour employment listings, and cold call aplenty. Play the numbers game. If push comes to shove, diverge from conventional thinking and consider alternative ways of catching on with frontline employers—think outside the box, and go after your future via other, novel plans of attack. Secure your spot with a top-flight employer by any means necessary.

Be relentless in the number of firms you canvass and the number of resumes you disperse. Telephone more employers, forge more connections, and send out more copies of your resume. Outclass your competition. Pursue as many top-tier firms on your radar as possible. Permit yourself no idle time. The more opportunities you go after, the greater your chances of hitting pay dirt. You only need to close one sale.

Sustain your thrust, and keep your operation moving forward at all times. Until you pull down your first real offer from an A-1 employer, refrain from thinking you have accomplished enough in terms of your effort or that after reaching out to a number of potential suitors and spreading around several copies of your resume, you have drained the opportunity well dry. You can always do more. You can always exert more energy and find a way to further promote your candidacy. Operate under the assumption that you can always find other companies to approach, other employment listings to forage through, and other connections to pin down. In the event you stall out or come up against momentum-derailing bottlenecks, keep your foot on the gas and shoot for progress, irrespective of the circumstances. If one door to opportunity slams shut, then simply pry open the next one. Never allow the job-search trail to grow cold. Stop at nothing.

Follow up with every lead. Stay in touch with every viable, or potentially viable, contact you connect with and every company representative or human resources personnel you start up dialogue with. Follow up with every resume submission you make, unless an employer behind an employment listing explicitly requests that all applicants refrain from doing so. Do not always wait to be called back. Do not always wait on your contacts or company point-persons to return your calls. Telephone them again. You can always make the next move. You never want to have a lead fizzle out or go nowhere because you dropped the ball or because you lacked in persistence. Until you receive a definitive "no" from the entities you give chase to, bend over backward to keep the conversation flowing. Seize the initiative. See every lead through to the end.

Never accept a position beneath your standards. If you genuinely covet a top-end, full-time post and the top-end paycheck that comes with it, set your sights on such an opportunity and do not settle for less. Catch on with an acceptable safety valve or fallback employer if your principal ambitions fail to pan out, provided such a move preserves the long-range integrity of your credentials, but under no circumstances come off your personal bar and compromise your future. Never take a short-term view, even in the face of job-search tribulation, and jeopardize your long-term prospects with upper-tier employers. Plant the seeds for a fruitful long-range career at the outset. Snare a promising, career-inaugurating opportunity that sets the table for a long, rewarding career.

With the specter of your job search looming large, take control of your future. In the face of an endless mountain of employers to approach, personal contacts to call on, new connections to forge, and resumes to disperse, set sail with no fear or reservation, and take advantage of the opportunity to nail down your spot within the upper ranks of the professional sphere.

The ball remains in your court. It's up to you to set up your future. It's up to you to answer the bell and find your way into a superlative firm. This is your opportunity to shine. This is your opportunity to cash your investment in your college education.

About the Author

Beginning as a know-nothing college student with no career expertise, but determined to land with a frontline employer after graduation, S. A. Eberwein discovered the keys to job search success. Mastering resume-writing, interviewing, and, ultimately, carrying out a productive job search after seeking out guidance from individuals in the upper echelon of the workforce, he parlayed his university degree into a highly sought-after investment banking position with an eminent, large-scale investment bank in New York City. After plying his trade in the hustle and bustle of Manhattan for five years, he moved back to his hometown of Dallas, Texas, where he currently resides with his wife and two small children. *Cash Your Investment* is his first book.